Restoring Thucydides

RESTORING THUCYDIDES

Testing Familiar Lessons
and
Deriving New Ones

Andrew R. Novo and Jay M. Parker

Rapid Communications in Conflict and Security Series
General Editor: Geoffrey R.H. Burn

CAMBRIA
PRESS

Amherst, New York

Requests for permission should be directed to
permissions@cambriapress.com, or mailed to:
Cambria Press
100 Corporate Parkway, Suite 128
Amherst, New York 14226, USA

Library of Congress Cataloging-in-Publication Data on file.

ISBN: 978-1-62196-474-2

*"My work is not a piece of writing designed to
meet the taste of an immediate public,
but was done to last forever."* —Thucydides, 1.22 (W)

***

*For all teachers, especially my mother and father,
who have worked to gain knowledge, and to share it.* —ARN

*For Corinne, who bore and endured this for so long.
And for Mom, who always knew this would happen.* —JMP

TABLE OF CONTENTS

Acknowledgements

This book was written while we served on the faculty of the College of International Security Affairs of National Defense University. It was not written incidental to our official responsibilities or during duty hours. The views expressed in this book are those of the authors and do not represent the views of the U.S. Department of Defense, National Defense University, or the College of International Security Affairs, or any other agency of the U.S. Government.

Our collective thanks to Geoffrey Burn and Toni Tan of Cambria Press for their encouragement, confidence, and extraordinary patience. The comments and advice of our anonymous reviewers helped focus the final draft. Thanks to the Cambria Press team, including David Armstrong for herding us through the final lap. Special thanks to Ila C. Bridges for her keen eye and sharp pencils. We gratefully acknowledge the intellect and insights of Chris Gregg who contributed so much to the early phases of this project, particularly in our first research presentation to the International Studies Association annual meeting. Thank you to our attentive discussants Mlada Bukovansky, Noel Anderson, Sarah Shoker, and to the audiences at our ISA presentations. We are honored and humbled by our many colleagues who have encouraged and critiqued us as we wrote this manuscript. Special thanks to Chris Bassford, Russ Burgos, Craig Deare, John Francis, Geoff Gresh, Sean McFate, Elena Pokalova, and Peter Thompson.

* * *

Thanks to friends, colleagues, and especially students at multiple institutions who have endured, bravely challenged, and most certainly sharpened and improved my rants on this topic for several decades. Thanks to Matt Hipple and Matt Merighi for providing me an early platform to test these views. My deep appreciation and special thanks to Thomas Sherlock and Scott Silverstone. Enduring thanks to Andrew Novo for getting me to finally shut up and put up. Most of all my inadequate thanks and unflinching love to Corinne, Kirsten, and Jeb who made this possible in more ways than I can count.

—JMP

* * *

Engaging with Thucydides remains enormously rewarding, not only because of the work itself, but because of the opportunity it presents to engage with so many colleagues who retain so much passion for a subject so familiar. To several of those colleagues, with whom I have discussed and debated Thucydides over the years, I owe a special debt of thanks: Nick Kenney, Elias Kouskouvelis, Athanasios Platias, Niall Ferguson, and of course, my co-author, Jay Parker. Special thanks are also due to Argyris Stringaris for our discussions on the finer points of ancient Greek vocabulary.

Finally, I would be remiss if I did not thank my family, my wife Natalie for her patience and my sons, Stephanos and Marcos, for their indulgence in their father's work at all hours of the day and night.

—ARN

A NOTE ON CITATIONS

We have consulted multiple translations of Thucydides in order to find common elements and, at a minimum, to present the reader with competing alternatives when the specific word choice is especially important. When citing these works, we do not rely on page numbers in the modern texts. Instead, we use the style consistent when dealing with ancient texts. Any references to portions of *The History* will include the book, paragraph, and—in the case of direct quotes—the translator's initials. For example, the citation for Warner's translation (Penguin 1954) —the primary translation used in our book—of Thucydides's explanation for the cause of war in Book 1, paragraph 23 will be given as Thucydides 1.23 (W) in the corresponding endnote. Other ancient texts are also cited based on book and paragraph. Ancient plays are cited by their relevant lines. A single translation of these works was used.

A Timeline of the Peloponnesian War

550 BCE Peloponnesian League formed by Sparta, Corinth, Elis, and Tegea

490 BCE Battle of Marathon, Athenian forces defeat the Persians

480 BCE Battle of Thermopylae, Spartan-led forces defeated by the Persians
Sack of Athens by the Persians

480 BCE Battle of Salamis, Athenian-led fleet destroys the Persian navy

479 BCE Battle of Plataea, Spartan-led coalition defeats remaining Persian forces in Greece

478 BCE Delian League formed, establishes treasury on Delos

469 BCE Naxos's attempt to leave the Delian League fails. Naxos enslaved

464 BCE Great Earthquake in Sparta and helot revolt

460 BCE First Peloponnesian War begins

458 BCE Treaty of cooperation between Athens and the Sicilian city state of Egesta

457 BCE Sparta defeats Athens at battle of Tanagra

454 BCE Delian League treasury moved to Athens

451 BCE Athens and Sparta agree to a five-year truce. Thirty Years Peace between Sparta and Argos

446 BCE Thirty Years Peace between Athens and Sparta begins

432 BCE Sparta claims Athens has broken Thirty Years Peace, Revolt of Potidaea begins

431 BCE Cycladic city-states side with Athens, Thebes sides with Sparta

431 BCE Spartan forces invade Attica for the first time

430 BCE Plague breaks out in Athens

429 BCE Pericles dies in plague

429 BCE Athens successful in Corinthian Gulf campaign

429 BCE Spartan siege of Plataea begins

428 BCE Revolt of Mytilene

427 BCE Plataea falls to Spartan forces

427 BCE First Athenian expedition to Sicily

425 BCE Athenian forces defeat Sparta in the naval engagement of Pylos

424 BCE Athenian expeditions against Megara and Boeotia fail

424 BCE Athenian forces defeat the Spartans on the island of Sphacteria. 120 Spartan peers are captured

423 BCE A one-year truce is agreed

422 BCE Sparta defeats Athens at Amphipolis.

421 BCE Peace of Nicias begins

418 BCE Sparta defeats the forces of Argos and Athens at Mantinea

417 BCE Melos attacked by Athens

415 BCE Athenian forces attack Sicily, following Alcibiades-Nicias debate in the Assembly

415 BCE Alcibiades charged with heresy and flees to Sparta

413 BCE Athens defeated in Sicily

412 BCE Sparta and Persia conclude an alliance

412 BCE Rhodes revolts against Athens, allies with Sparta

411 BCE Spartan forces resume operations against Athens

411 BCE Oligarchic coup in Athens topples the democracy and replaces it with the rule of the Four Hundred

411 BCE Rule of the Four Hundred replaced by the Five Thousand

410 BCE Alcibiades commands victorious Athenian fleet at Cyzicus

408 BCE Lysander made strategos of Spartan Fleet

407 BCE Alcibiades returns to Athens and selected as strategos

407 BCE Lysander commands victorious Spartan fleet at Notium

405 BCE Battle of Aegospotami, Spartan forces under Lysander destroy the Athenian fleet

404 BCE Sparta accepts the surrender of Athens after a brief siege. The Rule of the Thirty Tyrants begins in Athens

Restoring Thucydides

INTRODUCTION

THUCYDIDES LOST

"[H]ow little trouble most people take in their search for the truth —they happily resort to ready made opinions."[1]

—Thucydides

"It was written four hundred years before Christ and it talks about how human nature is always the enemy of anything superior. Thucydides writes about how words in his time have changed from their ordinary meaning, how actions and opinions can be altered in the blink of an eye. It's like nothing has changed from his time to mine."

—Bob Dylan[2]

More than 2500 years after it was written, Thucydides's book *The History*— his sole known work—is still read by academics, students, and policy-makers looking for enduring lessons in everything from grand strategy to domestic politics and human nature. With almost incredible frequency, Thucydides is cited (accurately or not) by scholars and students, poli-cymakers, and talking heads. His work is quoted in op-eds, Twitter feeds, and even the occasional screenplay. It has impressed philosophers, politicians, academics, and songwriters. His account of the Peloponnesian War (431–404 BCE)[3] has consistently been cited for its relative objectivity in recounting the actions of leaders and their states in a factual manner. But praise for Thucydides does not stop with recognizing his devotion to the facts and historical tradecraft. Thucydides has been hailed as the "most celebrated and admired" historian of war.[4] He retains a particular preeminence within international relations (IR) and strategic studies, and his influence goes far beyond those disciplines.

Thucydides's work has been recognized as significant since it was written. Excavations of ancient papyri have uncovered Thucydides side by side with Plato, the Bible, and the great plays of Athens, demonstrating his prominence within the classical "canon."[5] Literary references attest to Thucydides's importance throughout antiquity where his work remained a "seminal and popular text."[6] It served as both source and inspiration for a succession of historians, beginning with Xenophon and continuing through Polybius, Plutarch, and Cassius Dio to Procopius.[7] The style of the public speeches presented in Thucydides became a model for later audiences, either to praise or reject.[8] The political dilemmas the orators debated became the stock-in-trade of every classical teacher of rhetoric.[9]

Thucydides's salience to scholarship has endured over the centuries. In just the past five years, his iconic book has staked its claim on the future of international politics through the creation of an alleged "Thucydides's Trap"—a metaphor for the (almost) inevitable conflict between China and the United States.[10] Because of *The History*'s focus on state actors and great power politics interspersed with theoretical insights and philosophical analysis, the book serves as an *ur* text for international relations scholarship. Its contribution to understanding foreign policy decisions and the origins of war have proven particularly significant.

For hundreds of years, *The History* has remained a credible source of policy prescriptions for policymakers. Few books have had a wider, more sustained impact in bridging the gap between the academy and the policy world. Yet neither Thucydides's *History* nor interpretations stemming from it are above reproach. A tendency to treat his pronouncements on international politics as gospel is as flawed as it is dangerous. Appealing to Thucydides as a final word or untouchable foundation for theory is also problematic. This is because of both the nature of Thucydides's text and the manner in which we read it.

In this book, our goal is to push back against the oversimplification and decontextualization of Thucydides, both of which undermine the value of his work. There is no doubting that value, but it can only be realized if we look to understand both the context of his history and the history of his context. We must—as Thucydides himself admonishes his readers from the very start—avoid the easy "resort to ready-made opinions" to which we are all susceptible.[11] This means a deeper and more substantive engagement with:

1) Thucydides's text as a whole;
2) the context of Thucydides's time; and,
3) *The History* of the Hellenic world after the period covered in *The History*.

Such an approach holds the possibility of not only testing the veracity of various claims about the lessons supposedly within Thucydides but also providing new issues for consideration.

In the text that follows we will work across four principles, using our holistic approach to see where an appeal to broader evidence and argument can:

1) confirm the lessons attributed to Thucydides;
2) suggest that the standard interpretations give us *necessary* but not *sufficient* causes for actions in international relations;
3) contradict modern distillations;
4) make new ideas and debates possible.

This book is neither a historical treatise on previously unknown and unexplored facts nor a new contribution to the paradigms of international relations. Instead, we intend to demonstrate the value of historical context in engaging with major works used in the development of international relations theory. Only by understanding that context can theoretical keywords for Thucydides—we might start with "power" and "fear"— derive their meanings and therefore their theoretical power. Across seven chapters, this book will test four central concepts derived from Thucydides's work, which continue to exert a powerful influence on both scholars and policymakers:

1) the relationship of systemic structure to conflict (particularly bipolarity and its role in hegemonic transition theory);
2) the nature of "power" and "fear" as drivers of policy;
3) the role of domestic politics and the amoral exigencies of *realpolitik* in shaping foreign policy; and
4) the influence of alliances and alignment shifts on great power politics.

These concepts combine testing familiar Thucydidean lessons for their veracity with deriving potentially useful new ones.

In engaging with *The History*, it is not our intention to either confirm or disprove Thucydides's claims, nor are we seeking to overturn the theories that are built on his work. It is also not our intention to present definitive interpretations of various problems he presents. We hope that our exploration will provide grounds for additional debate and for the overarching principle that any study—particularly those of foundational texts—provides richer and more persuasive arguments if we embrace the complexity of our sources rather than streamline them for the sake of convenience.

This introduction lays out the foundations for that claim and presents some preliminary arguments about why and how Thucydides has often been misused. It concludes with the outline of the structure of the book. We will lay out the problems we believe exist in how Thucydides is read and argue that the reading of other foundational texts is likely to suffer from similar shortcomings. We will also offer some ideas on how to overcome these challenges.

Subsequently, chapter 1 will present a brief outline of the historical narrative presented in *The History* in order to familiarize readers with the various actors and chronology. It will continue with a brief description of Thucydides himself, before addressing aspects of the evolution of scholarly engagement with Thucydides and how his work is used as a teaching tool today in general terms. It will conclude by laying out five broad lessons often derived from Thucydides's text and contrast them with what we consider to be more sustainable interpretations. We will elucidate these through the rest of the book.

Chapter 2 will address the problems posed by the systemic interpretation of the causes of war as gleaned from Thucydides. This argument is dependent on a narrow interpretation (and particular translation) of one line in *The History*. For all its purported explanatory power, this systemic analysis relies on the identification of the Hellenic world as bipolar when, we shall argue, it was not. A systemic interpretation also fails to grapple with the complexities of the political and social conditions in both Athens and Sparta, all too often painting the two states as fundamentally antithetical. It ignores the critical role played by alliance structures in shaping foreign policy and conflict—which Thucydides addresses in other, neglected, sections of his work. Finally, a systemic explanation also overlooks the complex nature of power itself.

Chapter 3 builds on the critical problem of defining "power" to explore in detail the meanings of "power" and "fear" that are presented in the book. We look to reveal the complexities Thucydides presents about power and fear and how the broader scholarship about ancient Greece can help us understand these terms with specific reference to the actors in his account. We also look at how he applies those motivations to Athens, Sparta, and other major players in the Hellenic world in their decision-making processes. This, we argue, makes more coherent interpretations of Thucydides possible. We illustrate this through a focused analysis of what is probably the most famous line of Thucydides today—that the war between Sparta and Athens was caused by "the growth of Athenian power and the fear which this caused in Sparta."[12] Contrary to a simplified and stylized view of power, Thucydides presents an exploration of power that is complex and multilayered throughout his book. Thucydides's analysis on the complexity of power remain highly relevant. It demonstrates how power is difficult to measure and why it can be problematic to apply to achieving desired outcomes. Thucydides's text forces us to go beyond simplistic conceptions of the distribution of power within the international system and challenges us to think about how states view their own power and the power of their rivals, how material resources present both limitations and opportunities, and how the resources of a state—however great they may be—are always constrained by that state's domestic politics and institutions. These interpretations of power are critical to how leaders within states evaluate their national interests and make decisions based on that analysis.

Chapter 4 utilizes some of the least analyzed content from Thucydides to draw out important broader lessons about the nature of great power competition. We argue that this largely ignored material holds lessons beyond those traditionally attributed to Thucydides. Rather than portraying war and peace as driven primarily by the considerations of two dominant rivals, for example, Thucydides crafts a narrative of fluid alliances, diplomatic realignments, and conflict proceeding in fits and starts as rival domestic parties grappled for power. Modern scholars often frame the struggle between Athens and Sparta as one between a sea power (Athens) and a land power (Sparta). This is inconsistent with the reality that Athens had the largest (and one of the most effective) armies in the Greek world. At the start of the conflict, Sparta had few ships, but its allies possessed a large and effective fleet. Over the course of the war, Sparta built a large naval capability and eventually achieved victory over Athens through a series of naval engagements.

Chapter 5 takes the thread of decision-making and explores it within the context of domestic politics and the role of political realism in *The History*. Thucydides's realism, of course, is a notorious problem. Often the debate centers on the infamous Melian Dialogue (Book 5.84–116), a unique and far-reaching debate between representatives of the Athenians and the Melians. Thucydides's account is rich in its description and analysis of domestic politics, yet domestic politics are often overlooked as international relations scholars search for parsimony and focus on system-level analysis. Furthermore, those portions of Thucydides that do reinforce the ideas of realism do so with far more complexity and conditionality than normally cited. The Melian Dialogue, we argue, is no exception. Finally, in reporting on the expedition to Sicily, which immediately followed the events on Melos, Thucydides vividly shows us the potential costs and consequences of realist policies, while further demonstrating the importance of domestic politics.

Chapter 6 challenges the conclusions regarding the fallout from hegemonic wars and looks to draw more sustainable lessons instead. It utilizes Thucydides's analysis about great power conflict across *The History*, but also the events of the final years of the Peloponnesian War and the subsequent history of the Greek city-states. An account of these later events is not included in *The History*. As a result, modern scholarship often fails to consider this additional evidence. These events emphasize a continuing focus on the balance of power and the enduring nature of conflict even after the conclusion of hegemonic wars, which are conventionally viewed as fundamentally altering the nature of the system in favor of a peaceful equilibrium.

This book concludes with observations on continuity in international relations and an argument for the reexamination of other classics used to develop theories of IR and to support policy choices. Throughout, our aim will be to demonstrate the importance of handling Thucydides holistically. Our goal is to use his work as a basis to begin and to sustain a comprehensive examination of theory and prescription, rather than as a tool to simplify and avoid discussion. Thucydides provides conclusions, but he also provides enduring questions—questions we must not ignore in our quest for tidy answers.

THE PROBLEM

Like many great books, Thucydides's work is quoted too often and read too little. Even when it is read, like almost all great books, it is read in the search for predetermined lessons derived from preselected excerpts. When carefully studying where, when, and how Thucydides's work is cited, four significant problems are apparent. First—even in academic contexts—quotations from Thucydides are almost always stripped of their original rich, supporting context, so that they become little more than bromides.[13] When quotations are deracinated from the text and reduced to pithy sayings, they are deployed almost solely for the purpose of validating the author's arguments rather than to engage with the arguments presented by Thucydides. Instead of being a starting point for engagement, Thucydides's work is reduced to an exotic, sophisticated, and therefore unimpeachable source of support for a contemporary argument. His work derives its authority because it is so complex. But this complexity manifests itself in ambiguity and difficulty to read. Nevertheless, it "is invoked to support a simplistic, reductivist version of his alleged ideas." This tendency is what Neville Morley calls the "Thucydides paradox."[14] It is easy, for example, to read that "justice" means nothing more than that "the strong do what they have the power to do and the weak accept what they have to accept"[15] and for us to accept this as support for a coldly realist worldview, embracing power and shunning normative thinking. But we must look more deeply than that. What, for example, was the fate of the Athenians who made this appeal to the inherent justice of power? How does that account cohere to other evidence in Thucydides's work? Should we treat the Athenian commanders in Melos as simple ciphers for Thucydides's own ideas on the nature of international relations?

This highlights a second challenge in the reading of Thucydides—the frequent (and erroneous) attribution of everything in his book to him as if it expressed his views. It is perfectly reasonable, for example, to argue that Thucydides disagreed with the claims of the Athenian representatives in Melos regarding power and justice. His account could conceivably represent his understanding of what the Athenian representatives said, without endorsing it. The destruction of Melos and the subsequent expedition to Sicily were not necessarily policies Thucydides recommended, just what he had to record in order to accurately tell the history of events. There is room for genuine scholarly debate on this issue. Moreover, as readers, we should not have to take either reprobation or affirmation of the various speakers presented as Thucydides's unambiguous intent. Instead, we should look at his work in its entirety and craft our arguments and interpretations accordingly. We must acknowledge, as Morley argues, that complexity and ambiguity are integral to Thucydides and not lose sight of that in our pursuit of parsimony.

One manner to improve our interpretation is to better understand Thucydides's context. A third problem is that Thucydides is often approached in a vacuum that sucks away historical evidence about his period. The lessons drawn from his work are devoid of engagement with the historical period, which has important information for shaping our views. Readers take for granted the strength of Sparta, without looking deeper into Thucydides's text to uncover Sparta's significant weaknesses and to consider how those influenced its decisions of war and peace. We assume "the growth of Athenian power" was linear and unchecked, without testing available historical evidence both inside and beyond Thucydides to show that it was neither of those things. Both academics and policymakers use a sentence like "the truest cause of the war was the growth of Athenian power and the fear this caused in Sparta" to deduce that great power wars are caused when a rising power challenges a hegemon as a system characterized by a dominant power shifts to bipolarity. However, without referring back to the text and its context, it is difficult to comprehend the meaning of Athenian "power" or the actual basis of Spartan "fear."

How can we understand the catalyst of Spartan "fear" for the war with Athens if we know nothing about Spartan society, the nature of its political system, the structure of its alliance system, or the roots of its military power? These are essential elements if we are to understand what the Spartans were afraid of, beyond the simple (but not particularly helpful) claim that they felt fear. How can we understand whether the arguments of Sparta's allies would convince them to intervene against Athens without attempting to understand how Sparta's system of alliances functioned? There is no doubt that Spartan fear played a role in the war with Athens, but it was a necessary, not sufficient cause for the momentous war that began in 431. In engaging with the data Thucydides presents, we cannot be satisfied with the necessary. We must aim to uncover the sufficient as well. Otherwise, we uncover relatively little of value beyond broad generalizations, which are not supported in the wider text.

A failure to engage with the broader context of *The History* opens readers to another shortcoming—taking Thucydides purely at face value, without challenging the biases present in his work. Thucydides was an excellent historian and one praised for his historical methods, but this does not mean that his work is free from errors, contradictions, and even intentional distortions of the facts in order to serve his particular agenda. Where possible, we will engage with these issues as well, testing what we know against what Thucydides presents and seeing whether the result suggests different historical or theoretical conclusions. Testing the reliability and accuracy of Thucydides, as sacrilegious as this might seem to some, means exploring not only the evidence available in his book but also other ancient authors, archaeology, epigraphy, and modern scholarship on antiquity. Readers can greatly benefit from delving even further into layers of context. A small example of this would be to explore how *The History* of the Peloponnesian War is echoed in the work of the Athenian theater. The plays of ancient Athens, tragedies and comedies alike, contributed significantly to Athenian political life and provide another window into Athenian society. They celebrated great moments in the history of the Greek states, such as the wars with Persia, and overlaid contemporary issues on classical tales from mythology. In

Athens, at least, the theater—perhaps more than anywhere else—gave voice to dissent and doubt that was both uncensored and profound. It was a medium through which criticism could be leveled at Athenian policy in a mass audience in ways that political leaders often dared not present in their rhetoric for fear of exposing themselves to the fickle revenge of the Assembly.[16]

For example, Euripides's *The Suppliants*, performed in 423, excoriates the costs of war, sustaining an attack on its brutality through the tears and lamentations of mothers who have lost their sons. Euripides juxtaposes these obvious costs with the potential of war to humble arrogance and bring about (bloody) justice. The play is focused on the refusal of Thebes to allow for the burial and funeral rites of its enemies. This subject makes it a parable for the contretemps after the battle of Delium in which the Thebans initially refused to return to the Athenians their dead as recorded in Thucydides.[17] *The Suppliants* was written at a time after the ravages of the Athenian plague[18] and when the great battles of the first phase of the Peloponnesian War had inflicted huge losses and robbed both Athens and Sparta of their most hawkish leaders. Peace was in the air, and Euripides was obviously keen to grab it. His Theban herald also laments the fickleness of democracies declaring that when "the city has to vote on the question of war, no man ever takes his own death into account, but shifts this misfortune on to his neighbor; but if death had been before their eyes when they were giving their votes, Hellas would ne'er have rushed to her doom in mad desire for battle."[19] In this way, we see how contemporary literature provides an additional source of context for Thucydides's *History*.

Simplistic lessons also frequently avoid a deeper discussion of the course of the entire Peloponnesian War (the final seven years of which do not appear in *The History*), or the events that followed the surrender of Athens. That history (not recounted by Thucydides) is also useful evidence if we are to derive enduring lessons of value. For example, in practically his first sentence, Thucydides explains the division of the

Greeks into two warring sides, with every *polis* (city-state) joining either Sparta or Athens in the great struggle.[20] This claim, along with other elements of *The History*, has been used to demonstrate the bipolarity of the Hellenic world. Such a description is not only anachronistic but inaccurate and can be refuted with a wealth of evidence both in Thucydides's work and beyond his account.

Fourth, in turning a blind eye to Thucydides's broader time, we open ourselves to a damaging presentism. While ignoring history and context, we project the concerns of the present onto Thucydides's *History*. We see the rivalry between Athens and Sparta as an allegory for the Cold War competition between the United States and the Soviet Union[21] or, more frequently today, between the United States and China.[22] We define the conflict between Sparta and Athens narrowly and inaccurately as one between a land power and a sea power.[23] The failure of the Athenian expedition to Syracuse becomes an allegory for America's failure in Vietnam.[24] In the pages that follow we will demonstrate why such presentism creates damaging distortions rather than useful analogies.

Motivation is often part of the problem. Those who cite Thucydides frequently seek to impose their biases and perspectives on Thucydides. They want to appropriate him to use him as an authority to support *realpolitik* or to speak out against militarism, populism, or even democracy itself. They see Thucydides's work through the lens of their own time and derive what they want him to tell us about our own time rather than the general lessons Thucydides presented. To serve these ends, Thucydides's work is cut, pasted, and stretched to provide a direct connection to the present. His book is made timely at the cost of its timelessness.

These four common pitfalls are accelerated, and the adverse consequences are compounded, as contemporary tools like the Internet and social media confer unwarranted legitimacy on questionable resources and facilitate the confirmation bias that drives much of the online search process. While the Internet adds a new dimension and serves as a convenient scapegoat, the premises behind this challenge are old. Classic works and venerated authors suffered this fate long before the invention of modern information technology. Interpretations of Thucydides's work are typical of the use of similar classical historic accounts and political commentaries. Machiavelli and Clausewitz come immediately to mind as cases where complex ideas—deeply rooted in specific contexts—become bumper stickers. Generalizations drawn from long histories become analogies that perfectly intersect with the present. Debates over policies and options are called to a halt because the supporters of an argument can more readily attach a heroic and well-known personality to their argument. Ultimately, the error does not stop with the single initial case. The analogies are often reapplied after pruning and reshaping to fit another crisis between other nations at another time.

Soon the shorthand takes on its own identity and becomes representative of everything from long patterns of history to the idiosyncratic behavior of one individual. Over time, the shorthand's use depends more on the intent of its user than any empirical analysis. The original intent of the author is eroded in favor of the popular interpretation. For example, is "Machiavellian" being used as an insult, an endorsement, or merely as an objective description? Despite credible and empirically justifiable ways to use the term for all three, in practice it is most often a thinly considered, weakly defensible label of suspicion and disdain. Shorthands satisfy the needs of the present, but they do not convince. They silence debate through a simplistic but ultimately erroneous appeal to authority —in this case the authority of Thucydides.

Errors regarding his work are not confined to those who barely remember the name from a passing mention in an introductory-level college course. Distinguished scholars, senior government officials, educated journalists, and experienced policy analysts do the same. Three superficial examples can demonstrate the point:

1) Several years ago, the leadership of an international affairs organization considered a member's proposal to award a prize named for Thucydides. The suggestion was heatedly rejected by senior acad-

emics who refused to celebrate an author they saw as the unrepentant father of the worst excesses of realist thought.

2) The U.S. House Armed Services Committee once published a major study of professional military education that began with a full-page quotation from Thucydides in large typeface and impressive font. Thucydides never wrote the words.[25]

3) A prestigious research center at a major university posted a scene from the popular film Wonder Woman, noting favorably a discussion between the title character and German General Ludendorff:

> General Ludendorff (Danny Huston): "Peace is only an armistice in an endless war."
>
> Diana Prince/Wonder Woman (Gal Gadot): "Thucydides."
>
> Ludendorff: "You know your ancient Greeks."[26]

Unfortunately for Wonder Woman, Ludendorff, and audiences everywhere, once again, the quote did not come from Thucydides.

Beyond contemporary discourse, Thucydides's work underpins several continuous and critical tenets of international relations. Quotations from *The History* support foundational theories from classical realism to hegemonic transition theory. Oversimplified versions of Thucydides are presented in texts to undergraduates who, years later, reference remembered snippets in policy debates in spite of the fact that there are elements of a fuller interpretation that could better serve the building and application of theory and the making and analysis of policy. We can better understand the relationships between history and theory—and between theory and practice—through the construction and deconstruction of the narratives of war and peace that Thucydides presents. In so doing, we can validate the utility of interdisciplinary studies as a tool for exploring critical questions in international relations. Ultimately, an analysis of *The History* reaffirms the need to restudy other similar cases of misread, half-read, and unread writings. Any reading of his work, or similar core works, should be used as a foundation and starting point for discussion and not as an incontrovertible assertion designed to shut down debate.

OUR PURPOSE AND OUR METHOD

As authors, we represent differing and often contending disciplines. One of us is a student of classics and of history with graduate degrees from a British university. The other is a social scientist and international relations scholar with an exclusively American education. Over the course of many discussions, agreements, and arguments, we have realized that these distinctions in our background could serve as a strength in exploring this topic. As noted, the missteps we identified above are common; their subjects are not limited to one book by one author. Similar shortcomings and oversights are undoubtedly present in our own work. Our purpose here is to use the classic (and solitary) work of a single author as a means to explore how all of us—students, teachers, policymakers, pundits, and everyday citizens—use foundational texts to think about, interpret, and act on a complex, confusing, volatile, and insecure world.

In this book, we challenge and test several of the standard lessons derived from Thucydides based on the evidence within his work and the broader historical record. Next, using those same sources, we demonstrate how more comprehensive lessons can be drawn. We argue that a richer understanding of Thucydides is possible through a more complete reading of his work and the use of other available evidence. The clichés generated by current approaches do not help us understand the particular causes, conduct, and conclusion of the conflict between Athens and Sparta any more than they provide insights into the challenges of our own time.

This book does not exhaustively translate *The History*. There are sufficient, demonstrably accurate translations already available. Various translations have their merits, and there is appropriate scholarly debate concerning their accuracy. At times, we will present arguments for why a particular translation might better capture the sense of an argument, particularly where contemporary scholarship places a great reliance on the precise word Thucydides is supposed to have used; but analysis of such semantics is not our primary purpose here. Our book is not a presentation or interpretation of previously undiscovered and unreported archeological or archival evidence. Nor is it a presentation of new theories of international relations, or an attempt to sweep away earlier theories relying on Thucydides. We are concerned with how and on what evidentiary basis existing theories are developed. Existing theories may well hold up under reexamination after reading and accounting for our findings. Some theories may ultimately find greater support for their conclusions based on clearer, more accurately applied evidence.

This book is about the use and misuse of historical evidence. It is about the persistence of historical fact that has been surpassed by legend. It is about the search for continuities and predictability, and how that search goes astray in the absence of consistent, diligent, interdisciplinary scholarship. Important distinctions are lost between variables that are among many interdependent necessaries, and those rare variables that are solely and completely sufficient. Weak links are forged on the most tenuous of connections when stronger, more valuable links can be made with more comprehensive, contextual research. Ultimately, the analogies relied on for one crisis bleed over into the next. Imperfect lessons get dragged along in the wake, compounding the original error. This is not news. The problem of analogies and "lessons" from history has been studied almost as long as there has been history. Sometimes the offenders are relying on inaccurate or inadequate accounts of events. In other instances, confirmation bias is to blame for history being bent to conform to existing opinions. The causes are complex, but they certainly bear repeating.[27] When half-relevant quotes lend legitimacy to a weak argument or stop debate rather than spur further inquiry, the consequences can be tragic.

We will not fully, exhaustively explore every event, every actor, and every outcome presented by Thucydides. Instead, we have chosen a limited number of cases within *The History* that frequently appear in general introductory texts, in theoretical scholarship, and in public-policy arguments. We then examine these cases, asking whether their lessons are present in the text, fully supported by the full text, and credible given the broader, known context.

At first glance, our book may appear to be an attempt to directly rebut Graham Allison's appropriation of this ancient work as inspiration for *Destined for War: Can America and China Escape Thucydides's Trap?* published in 2017. Books like Allison's give false impressions about the causes of conflict and inaccurate frameworks through which to understand dynamics among major powers. Based as they are on such incomplete and unstable foundations, we believe that their prescriptions for policymakers will be similarly flawed. Allison's work is certainly timely, and we hope what we provide enhances and enlightens the debate his book has generated. However, our book is not meant to be a point-by-point rebuttal of "Thucydides's Trap" or its author. We strongly disagree with much of Allison's analysis and many of his conclusions. Some of those disagreements will be aired here. However, our arguments extend beyond one specific book, the conclusion it reaches, and the policy recommendations it offers.

Instead, our target is any reduction of a complex, detailed account of important events to a few buzz phrases that cannot be convincingly drawn from the book it cites. There is always a possibility that the conclusions drawn about this so-called trap ultimately, and serendipitously, align with US-China relations in the coming decades. If there is a trap, it is one woven with analogies that are weak and false. It is built on short, crisp, repeatable lessons that have drifted far from their origins. It is shaped to conform to expectations and to confirm conclusions that predate research. It is a common trap, not confined to the reading of Thucydides or the study of China. Our charge to readers is to use our findings and apply our methodology in order to question and, if need be, restructure assumptions—both their own and those of other scholars and policymakers. By doing so, they can better reexamine existing theories and interpretations and, perhaps, develop new ones of greater utility.

NOTES

1. Thuc. 1.20 (H)
2. Bob Dylan, *Chronicles: Volume I*, New York: Simon and Schuster, 2004, p. 36.
3. All dates are BCE unless otherwise stated.
4. Zagorin, *Thucydides*, 1.
5. Hornblower, Spawforth, and Eidinow, *The Oxford Classical Dictionary*, 691–692.
6. S. Kennedy, "A Classic Dethroned," 607.
7. Ibid., 609.
8. Fromentin and Gotteland, *A Handbook on the Reception of Thucydides*, 17.
9. S. Kennedy, "A Classic Dethroned," 610.
10. See, for example, Allison, *Destined for War*.
11. Thuc. 1.20 (H).
12. Thuc. 1.23 (W).
13. There are even instances where quotations are entirely misattributed or are reported so inaccurately that they cannot be properly identified as coming from Thucydides. We will not spend much time on these factual errors but will point out one or two occasions where they have occurred.
14. Morely, "The Melian Dilemma," 1.
15. Thuc. 5.89 (W).
16. The Athenian Assembly, or ἐκκλησία (ekklesia), was the principle assembly of the Athenian state where almost all matters of policy were debated. All citizens (males of appropriate age and lineage) sat in the Assembly and it had the final say in all legislation.
17. Thuc. 4.97–101.
18. The precise pathogen of the plague is still the subject of debate. Smallpox, bubonic plague, hemorrhagic fever (Ebola), typhus, and typhoid fever have all been considered possibilities.
19. Euripides, *Suppliants*, 484–484.
20. Thuc. 1.1.
21. Gaddis, *The Long Peace*, 221.
22. Allison, *Destined for War*.
23. Hanson, *A War Like No Other*, 6.
24. Turner, "Address to Chicago Council Navy League."

25. The quote, which has been often repeated and favorably highlighted by many other institutions and individuals reads, "The nation that will insist upon drawing a broad line of demarcation between the fighting man and the thinking man is liable to find its fighting done by fools and its thinking done by cowards." The actual source is the biography *Charles George Gordon*, by Colonel Sir William F. Butler (London and New York: MacMillan and Company, 1889) and can be found on page 85.
26. "Thucydides Takes Hollywood," Belfer Center for Science and International Affairs, Harvard University, https://www.belfercenter.org/thucydides-trap/book/wonder-woman.
27. Brands and Suri, eds., *The Power of the Past*; Neustadt and May, *Thinking in Time*; Khong, *Analogies at War*.

CHAPTER 1

TRAP OR TALISMAN?

"Mighty indeed are the marks and monuments of our empire which we have left. Future ages will wonder at us, as the present age wonders at us now."[1]

—Pericles

"[A]mong Greek historians Thucydides is like porphyry compared to other marbles or gold compared to metal in general."[2]

—Lorenza Valla

A MAN, HIS STATE, AND WAR

Having said that we will not exhaustively retell Thucydides's work as a narrative, it is still important to at least provide readers with a synopsis of both the work and the historical period as well as some basic facts about its author. This will be useful for those who have not read Thucydides since their student days, for those who have only read snippets as portions of a lesson assignment, and for those who have never read the book itself at all, as well as for those who lack a knowledge of the period he describes. Hopefully, it will send readers back to the original source, even if only to dispute what we write.

Put very briefly, Thucydides wrote a narrative and analytical history of a conflict that shook the Hellenic world between 431 and 404. The *poleis* (city states) of Athens and Sparta were the protagonists in this conflict. But, as we will show—and as Thucydides was quick to record—the war went far beyond these two actors. Both Athens and Sparta were the dominant members of alliances that included many other key *poleis*. The Athenians led what modern historians call the Delian League. Sparta and its allies composed what modern historians call the Peloponnesian League.

Over the course of the war, a number of neutral states, including several of significant size, came off the sidelines. These smaller states could be caught up in the violence through the aggression of the lead actors. At other times, they chose to enter the conflict to further their own foreign policy goals. Athens used an appeal for help from allies in Sicily to launch a campaign of conquest against Syracuse at the western limits of the Hellenic world. Athens suffered a catastrophic defeat in Sicily. As a result of this defeat, it soon confronted revolt in its empire, renewed operations by Sparta, and the intervention of the mighty Persian Empire on the side of Sparta. Through its satraps (provincial governors) along the coast of Asia Minor, the Persians supplied ships and money to the Spartans, eventually giving them the upper hand against the Athenians. The new Spartan fleet, crewed from across the Greek world and supported by Persian money, eventually defeated the Athenian fleet. Spartan land forces then laid siege to the city of Athens while its navy blockaded the Athenian port of Piraeus. On the brink of starvation, the Athenians agreed to surrender, ending the Peloponnesian War.

Sparta's Peloponnesian League was, in fact, a set of bilateral alliances made between Sparta and its neighbors in the Peloponnese. Some of these were tiny *poleis* with no real independence. Some were larger political entities that maintained control of their domestic politics and voted within the assemblies of the Peloponnesian League. Under the terms of their various agreements with Sparta, less-than-independent allies were usually required to "have the same friends and enemy as the Spartans" and "follow the Spartans withersoever they may lead by land and by sea."[3] Other allies, like Corinth, were major powers in their own right and maintained effective control over both their foreign and domestic policy. They could oppose Spartan policies if they chose, and they often did.

For the sake of clarity, we should note here that Spartan is a highly specific term, usually used to refer to the inhabitants of the city of Sparta itself who enjoyed the full privileges of citizenship. Thucydides uses the word Spartiate to describe this narrow category. It comes from the central urban settlement of Sparta itself. In addition, Thucydides uses the word Lacedaemonian. The city of Sparta was the capital of the region called Lacedaemon or Laconia. Lacedaemon referred to the Spartan *polis* as a political unit—something larger than the urban settlement itself— making the terms Sparta and Lacedaemon essentially interchangeable. The key difference is that Spartan would refer to only those with the full privileges of citizenship whereas Lacedaemonian could refer to those who were individually free but nevertheless lacking fully equal status in Spartan society.

Outsiders, like Thucydides, found it notoriously difficult to understand the many layers of Spartan society and modern historians share some of their confusion. Even contemporaries with some experience of Sparta found it confusing. Thucydides also uses the word "Peloponnesian." In his work, this refers generally to any of the city-states of the Peloponnesian peninsula who were allied to Sparta. As a result, the terms Spartan and Peloponnesian are not interchangeable. All Spartans were from the Peloponnese, but not all Peloponnesians were Spartans. Nor were all Peloponnesians even allied with Sparta. Argos, for example, was the second-largest political entity in the Peloponnese and famous Spartan rival. Finally, we should note that not all of Sparta's allies came from the Peloponnese. Some members of the Peloponnesian League, as Thucydides records, came from as far away as Sicily.[4] This complex social structure of Sparta and its allies will be elaborated on in chapter 3 and is essential to understanding the essence and exercise of Spartan power.

In contrast to Sparta, Athens's Delian League was largely an imperial construction. Created during the Persian Wars (499–446 BCE), the league allowed Athens to dominate its immediate region and control the foreign policy, trade, and even domestic politics of numerous *poleis*, particularly among the islands of the Aegean Sea. For example, *poleis* within the Delian League had to submit most legal disputes to Athenian courts. Over time, the Athenian position within the league shifted from that of first among equals to a dominant metropole extracting tribute and troop contributions. These ships, soldiers, and tribute were used, as intended, to fight the Persians but progressively to serve Athenian interests. As the years passed, numerous *poleis* began to make their contributions in purely financial terms, allowing Athens to hire ships and men on their behalf. This, naturally, made Athens progressively more powerful as it came to control the military resources of most Greek states within the Aegean, along with a substantial amount of their financial resources. Nothing symbolized this evolution of cooperative alliance to Athenian "empire" more clearly than the transfer of the league's treasury from the island of Delos (hence the name Delian League) to Athens in 454. Imperialist policies turned Athens into a major trading and political hub. Huge revenues flowed into the city from trade duties and tribute. This wealth and power launched the so-called Golden Age of Athens in which it produced architectural, artistic, and intellectual achievements that are still admired. During this period, it also experimented with a more broad-based political order called democracy.

Athenian democracy was innovative (its detractors called it radical) because of two essential factors. First, it was a direct democracy. All citizens (adult males who met property and lineage qualifications) voted on policy measures within the city's assembly, the *Ekklesia*. There were almost no checks or balances on the will of the voting public as expressed through this assembly. Beyond voting, citizens were expected to take an active role in the life of the city. They not only debated (and voted) on policy but sat on juries and served in public office. Every position in the Athenian state, from the lowest official planning a festival to the senior magistrates of the state, were chosen by lot from among the citizenry. The only exception to this practice of choosing by lot was the annual board of ten generals. These generals, due to the important nature of their work, were elected. As in the case of Thucydides himself, generals were typically chosen from among the richest and most influential families. Elite families not only exerted a powerful political influence over the city but also provided their sons with the best education and training available. The education of an Athenian youth had three pillars: academics, music, and physical education. Academic studies were focused on rhetoric, law, mathematics, science, and philosophy. As part of their musical instruction, Athenian youths would learn to sing and to play the flute or lyre. There was also a rigorous physical education from which the modern sports of track and field derive, including: running, jumping, throwing javelin and discus, wrestling, and boxing. Such skills, of course, represented the pursuit of physical excellence, but they also imbued an Athenian youth with the foundations of military skill. Members of the elite would also learn to ride.

The second characteristic that made Athenian democracy radical was that the definition of citizenship—forming the basis of politics—was liberal by the standards of the Hellenic world. There were restrictions based on birth—Athenian citizenship, for example, was eventually circumscribed to the legitimate offspring of two Athenian parents—but there were no restrictions based on property or wealth as was the case in almost every other *polis*. This meant that even poor Athenian citizens had a voice in their country's politics and a role to play in those politics.[5]

In Sparta, by contrast, citizenship was dependent on all the conditions present in Athens in addition to a financial hurdle requiring Spartiates to meet a threshold for contributions to their *syssitia* (common mess halls). This financial requirement reflected a society that enforced inequality along both social and economic lines. Financial impediments to citizenship made Sparta an oligarchy—a political system in which power rested in the hands of *o ligos* (the few), rather than one in which power rested in the hands of the many. As a result, Sparta, "more than... any other Greek state," was characterized by "a real and bitter class war."[6] Such class conflict was what the Athenian democracy was meant to avoid; but in giving power to the many, the system did create vulnerabilities to oligarchic reaction, as we shall see.

In spite of their differing approaches to citizenship and domestic governance, Athens and Sparta presented a united front of opposition to the Persian imperialism during the Persian Wars, which dominated Greek political life during the first three decades of the fifth century. During much of this period, Athens and Sparta were allies, working in concert against Persian attempts to put the city-states of Greece under their control. Readings of *The History* confined to the period between 431 and 404 do not take this long period of cooperation into account. Equally, it omits periods of earlier animosity. Between 460 and 445 the two erstwhile allies fought each other in a conflict called the First Peloponnesian War. Thucydides offers a truncated account of this conflict, but it remains in his text nonetheless. This war ended in a negotiated settlement called the Thirty Years Peace. By its terms, the clients of both Athens and Sparta were formalized. Allies of one state were forbidden from shifting to the other. Neutrals, however, could be welcomed into their respective leagues by either Athens or Sparta. Both Athens and Sparta were supposed to submit their disagreements to arbitration.

These terms were meant to establish a lasting peace. Within each state there were supporters of accommodation and cooperation. They favored what historians have called a "dual hegemony."[7] Under this concept, Sparta would maintain dominance within the Peloponnese. Athens would maintain its league and naval empire. Each would respect the international politics or domestic affairs of the other. This balance was precarious because there were groups within each state—and also members of Sparta's own alliance—who did not believe in the fundamental aspects of this compromise. These underlying tensions meant that a seemingly minor issue could quickly become a major international crisis.

Thucydides begins his account of the war with that crisis. In 435–433 there was a civil war in the frontier city of Epidamnus.[8] Such internecine conflicts were common throughout the Hellenic world. Often, they were the result of competition for power between oligarchs and democrats. In Epidamnus, the democrats were defeated. They fled and appealed to their mother city of Corcyra (modern Corfu) for aid. Corcyra, in turn, was a colony of Corinth (Sparta's most powerful ally). Corcyra and Corinth possessed particular characteristics that made them extremely relevant to the international politics of the Hellenic world. Corcyra possessed the third-largest navy in the Hellenic world. More importantly, it was an unaffiliated *polis*, part of neither the Athenian Delian League nor the Spartan Peloponnesian League. Geographically, the island stood astride the route from the Greek peninsula to Italy and the colonies in the West. This was particularly important considering the wealth in grain and timber available in southern Italy and Sicily along with other trading opportunities.

When the Corcyraeans refused the request for aid, the Epidamnian democrats appealed to Corinth. Corinthian leaders felt that Corcyra had not shown them the respect due their position as the founder of the colony and so were willing to help the Epidamnian exiles.[9] Corinth sent aid and restored the Epidamnian democrats to power. This caused a violent reaction in Corcyra, which now demanded the restoration of the deposed oligarchs and the expulsion of Corinthian troops and settlers. When these demands were refused, the Corcyraeans began military operations against Epidamnus and the supporting Corinthian forces.

A local disturbance was escalating quickly. Corinth now prepared a larger relief expedition and refused Corcyraean offers to take the matter to mediation. The Corinthian expedition was defeated. When Corinth threatened to return with a larger and more powerful force, the Corcyraeans appealed to Athens for support. This appeal put the Athenians in an awkward position. They were at peace with Corinth's largest ally, Sparta, under the terms of the Thirty Years Peace. Upsetting this momentous agreement would have enormous reverberations throughout the Hellenic world. At the same time, the crisis developing between Corcyra and Corinth represented a critical consideration for Athenian policymakers. Corcyra, a powerful neutral, was offering them an alliance while at the same time, a rival, Corinth, appeared poised to expand its power significantly if Athens did nothing.

After laborious deliberations, Athens agreed to a defensive alliance with Corcyra. This would oblige either party to defend the other in event of attack by a hostile third actor. It did not require either the Athenians or the Corcyraeans to join the other in offensive operations in an attack against another *polis*. To seal the arrangement, ten Athenian ships were sent to defend Corcyra from the impending Corinthian intervention, with orders that they were only to engage Corinthian forces if they threatened to invade the island itself. The ensuing naval battle, at Sybota (433), was a tactical draw, but the Corinthians were unable to land at Corcyra. The Athenian ships, constrained by their vague rules of engagement, hung back during the early stages of the battle before, perhaps inevitably, becoming fully embroiled in the struggle. During the closing stages of the engagement, an additional twenty Athenian ships arrived. These had been sent as an afterthought in support of the first contingent. Wary of the appearance of new Athenian forces, the Corinthians withdrew. The Corcyraeans also withdrew to lick their wounds. Both sides claimed victory.

Shortly after these events, Potidaea, a city that was part of the Delian League, but nevertheless a Corinthian colony, attempted to revolt from Athenian control. Athenian forces were sent to besiege Potidaea. In response, the Corinthians gathered a relief army. Critically, the Corinthian state did not deploy its forces to aid its colony. Instead, Corinth raised "a force of volunteers from Corinth itself and of mercenaries from the rest of the Peloponnese" for the confrontation in Potidaea.[10] Corinthian hesitation likely stemmed from the Corinthians' view that Potidaea would in all probability be lost (and so they wanted to minimize their losses), their belief that the city bore responsibility for its own defense, and, perhaps most critically, its uncertainty regarding Spartan support in the event of an open break with Athens.

Outside the walls of Potidaea, the Athenian army defeated the relief force in 432. In the wake of this second clash between Athenian and Corinthian forces, the Corinthians, with some difficulty, were able to convince the Spartans that the Athenians had violated the terms of the existing peace treaty between Sparta and Athens. Sparta declared the treaty broken and declared war on Athens. In 431, Spartan forces marched into the Athenian homeland, Attica, devastating crops and attempting to bring the Athenian army to battle. The Athenians refused this provocation and retreated behind the safety of their Long Walls—fortifications around the city of Athens itself and connecting the city of Athens to its port at Piraeus. The conflict would rage, on and off, for the next twenty-seven years, before the Spartans defeated Athenian forces, including their famous navy, and forced the surrender of the city in 404.

Although often enormously detailed, Thucydides's account of the war is incomplete. Although he did live long enough to witness the end of the conflict, he died before he could finish his work. His account ends midway (and mid-sentence) through the year 411. Critical events, foremost the conclusion of the war, are not covered. His proximity to events and the timing of his death meant that he had no long-term perspective on the war's impact. To better understand his work, it is also useful to provide some background to Thucydides himself.

Born around the year 465, we must remember that, first and foremost, Thucydides was a member of the Athenian elite. He was a citizen of the upper class, who came from significant personal wealth. He may have been related to leaders within the oligarchic party in Athens: Miltiades (the victor of Marathon) and his son, Cimon.[11] Thucydides's family owned the rights to rich gold mines in the northern region of Thrace. This region had an added strategic importance, lying along the route of the Athenian importation of grain from the Black Sea. Due to his wealth and family position, Thucydides would have been deeply engaged in the rich cultural life of Athens—rubbing elbows with the famous playwrights, poets, philosophers, and politicians who defined and created the city's "Golden Age." Chief among Athenian political leaders during this period was Pericles, who dominated Athenian politics between 460 and his death in 429, often serving as one of the city's ten elected *strategoi* (generals; singular *strategos*). He figures prominently in Thucydides's account. The son of a noted general, Pericles was also a highly skilled orator.[12] His mother was a member of the famous and wealthy Alcmaeonid family, a relative of the democratic reformer Cleisthenes. This made Pericles, by both talent and lineage, one of the most important figures in Athens.

Thucydides's relationship with Pericles is complex. While *The History* paints an admiring and sympathetic picture of the *strategos*, Thucydides is less sympathetic to the democratic policies championed by Pericles. Although he was also a member of the city's most prominent elite, Pericles was a thorough democrat who favored increased political rights and participation from the lower classes of the citizenry. Like many Athenian intellectuals, Thucydides remained skeptical of both democracy as a form of government and of Pericles's commitment to rule by the people. To Thucydides, under Pericles, what was "nominally a democracy" was really the rule of "the first citizen [Pericles]."[13] This analysis may be one reason Thucydides, who was not particularly fond of democracy, nevertheless found room to admire Pericles. While the Athenian political system functioned under Pericles' unique talents, Thucydides argued that his inferior successors "adopted methods of demagogy which resulted in their losing control over the actual conduct of affairs."[14] In Thucydides's view, the inherent vulnerability of the general populace to the appeal of demagogues—and their subsequent vicissitudes in mood and policy— was one of democracy's greatest shortcomings.

In 425, like Pericles before him, Thucydides was elected as one of the ten *strategoi*. As a *strategos*, Thucydides was assigned to a command in the north (probably because of his family connections in the region) on the island of Thasos. When the Spartan commander Brasidas laid siege to the coastal town of Amphipolis, the Athenian garrison sent to Thucydides at Thasos for aid. He arrived too late to relieve the city. He was removed from command shortly thereafter and exiled for his failure in the campaign.[15]

Thucydides's exile gave him both the time and opportunity to travel and to begin gathering material for *The History* he then decided to write. His account drew on his own observations and on the insights of others. He had the means to travel throughout the Hellenic world, gathering data from eyewitnesses as he did. He had his own opinions and conclusions, but he tried to be as objective as he could, even if that required criticism of actions he endorsed or even took. For example, he did not suppress his failure to relieve Amphipolis or his subsequent dismissal from his command.

In writing *The History,* Thucydides used a number of specific literary devices. Most prominently, he recorded a number of orations by leaders from all sides. He often framed them in debates between competing viewpoints as state leaders struggled to make and execute policy. This technique serves as a basis for misattribution. Many quotations attributed to Thucydides are, in fact, his reports of statements by other historic figures of the day. In many instances, the favorably presented saying of Thucydides is instead an assertion made by Pericles or another key player. A reading in the original context—particularly within the original debate—shows that Thucydides himself did not make the statement. More importantly, it is also apparent, in many cases, that he disapproved of the sentiments presented. In some instances, his intent is even to show the error of the speaker.

Thucydides himself admitted the limitations of his methodology regarding speeches. At the beginning of *The History,* he clearly explains two different sources for the speeches in the text. First, there were those he witnessed and wrote down as best he remembered them. Second, there were those he did not hear but which had been reported to him by individuals who had heard them. In both cases, however, he admitted that it was impossible to remember the speeches word for word and so he interpolated what, in his opinion, he thought the occasion demanded of the speaker.[16] It is therefore critical to remember that any speech in *The History* does not represent the words of the speaker but is Thucydides's interpretation of the speaker's intent. Moreover, the individuals whose thoughts and actions Thucydides reports are not presented merely as orators. Thucydides puts them in the context of their broader societies, personalities, and actions. There is little in the way of predetermined, unitary state action. Policies are debated; past actions are critiqued; human strengths and frailties are noted.

The world in which these events occur is dynamic and often unstable, both within and between these states. While the gods on Olympus are neither blamed nor praised, the role played by ancient faiths, traditions, and rituals remains prominent. Choices are made and actions taken for reasons ranging from logic to passion to superstition. Battles are fought or bypassed based on the readings of goat entrails. The environment gets a vote. Winds and tides, plagues and harvests all play their part, sometimes to devastating effect.

Finally, Thucydides's own death before completing his history prevented him from bringing his narrative to the end of the war and from drawing final conclusions. Statements within the text indicate that he did witness the end of the war, although we cannot know for certain when (or if) he returned to Athens itself. It is possible that he was recalled along with many other exiles in 411 during the rule of "the Five Thousand"—a government he praises.[17] This government was only in power briefly, before the return of the democracy. After Sparta's victory in 404, another general amnesty for Athenian exiles was promulgated, and it is also possible that Thucydides returned to Athens at this time. The scanty evidence we have suggests that he died shortly thereafter.

PLACING AND MISPLACING THUCYDIDES

Thucydides has a long and deep history of influencing scholarship. After the end of the Western Roman Empire at the end of the fifth century CE, Thucydides remained part of the Greek canon in the Byzantine East for the next three hundred years. By the eighth century CE, changes in style and worldview began to relegate his work to the reading lists of only the most arcane of antiquarians and students of rhetoric. His reputation rebounded somewhat in the twilight of Byzantium during the fourteenth and fifteenth centuries CE.[18] Increased intellectual contacts between the Latin West and the Greek East during the Italian Renaissance spurred a renewed interest in classical texts. The noted scholar Lorenzo Valla (who played a central role in the creation of the Vatican library) completed the first "modern" translation of Thucydides into Latin from the original Greek in 1452 CE on a commission from the Nicholas V, who was well known for his support of humanism and scholarship. Valla was certainly an admirer of both Thucydides's substance and style. In his inscription to the Pope, Valla wrote glowingly:

> among Greek historians Thucydides is like porphyry compared to other marbles or gold compared to metal in general. He possesses such dignity, such force, such credibility without blemish—which is most important in a historian—that readers never doubt the truth of his reports.[19]

Naturally, Valla's edition influenced and was influenced by the dynamics of the Italian Renaissance. Nearly two centuries after being translated into Latin, Thucydides's work was translated into English by none other than the great English philosopher Thomas Hobbes. As with Valla's account, Hobbes's translation had its own context. Published in 1629, Hobbes's translation of Thucydides pre-dates his *Leviathan* by almost twenty years. Influence from Thucydides is present in Hobbes' own work. For example, Hobbes' foundational formulation from *Leviathan* that "quarrel" has "three principal causes," "competition... diffidence... [and] glory,"[20] is paraphrased from Thucydides who ascribes the motivation of Athens's empire builders to "fear... honor and self-interest."[21] In a word, Hobbes's "realism" is thought, by many, to follow from the realism laid out in Thucydides.

Today, Thucydides remains widely influential in the study of international relations. His work is widely quoted in both textbooks and major works in the field. Thucydides's ideas—cut and chopped in myriad ways—are presented to students of history and politics in a variety of introductory texts. In some instances, limited portions of the original book are presented in textbooks with varying degrees of context.[22] However, normally a limited number of summary sentences are provided to reinforce the author's point. Joseph Nye uses Thucydides to illustrate several elements of realism (2009), to include the security dilemma and patterns of alliance behavior. In addition to providing a lengthy summary of Thucydides's book, he also cites book 2, chapter 65 as an example of IR works that demonstrate the recurring value of cases like the Peloponnesian War. Dunne, Kurki, and Smith view Thucydides's work as the origin for the "tradition of classical realism" including the work of Hans Morgenthau and E.H. Carr.[23] Art and Jervis also rely on Thucydides to frame the recurring elements of realism.[24] Dougherty and Pfaltzcraff, Jr. also use the oft-repeated Thucydidean argument that Sparta's fear of Athens's growing power was the cause of the war, then cite the Peloponnesian War as a realist analogy for the causes of World War I.[25] In a break with orthodoxy, Dougherty and Pfaltzcraff give Thucydides credit for illustrating key variables of decision-making theories.[26]

How Thucydides has influenced IR as a discipline remains something of a cottage industry. *Thucydides' [sic] Theory of International Relations: A Lasting Possession*, edited by Lowell Gustafson (2000), explores Thucydides's impact on international relations theory, ethics in international relations, morality, and empire, as well as the impact of democracy on foreign policy. Thucydides is prominent in major theoretical works in international relations. Richard Ned Lebow's *The Tragic Vision of Politics: Ethics, Interests, and Orders* (2003), Michael Doyle's *Ways of War and Peace* (1997), and Robert Gilpin's *War and Change* (1981) all have lengthy discussions of Thucydides. In Kenneth Waltz's *Man, the State, and War* (1959) Thucydides predates Machiavelli as the foundational text for *realpolitik*.[27] Waltz again cites Thucydides (this time a bit more benignly) in *Theory of International Politics* (1979), noting how from Hobbes to the present day, this account of the Peloponnesian War has led scholars to see continuities between the past and the present, particularly in the enduring dilemma of using and controlling force.[28]

In his comprehensive argument for offensive realism, *The Tragedy of Great Power Politics* (2001), John Mearsheimer dismisses bandwagoning as "a strategy for the weak." To reinforce his point, Mearsheimer notes, "Thucydides' [sic] famous dictum that 'the strong do what they can, the weak suffer what they must.'"[29] Later in the same text, Mearsheimer uses Thucydides to reinforce the longevity of realism as the preferred paradigm in international relations theory.[30] Dan Caldwell and Robert E. Williams, Jr, use the same quote to provide a counter to realism. Citing the Arab Oil Embargo of the 1970s, Caldwell and Williams argue that this event had "turned Thucydides on his head," by allowing the "weak" to dominate the "strong."[31]

Such debates highlight the need for caution in approaching Thucydides. A few noted IR scholars have attempted to provide more careful and nuanced discussions of Thucydides. For example, *A Handbook to the Reception of Thucydides*, edited by Christine Lee and Neville Morley, calls for reading Thucydides's work comprehensively. It engages with how each society reading Thucydides has interpreted it to suit its own needs and explain its own challenges. It looks specifically at how Thucydides has been read and received over time from the classical world through the Renaissance to modern explorations of Thucydides's influence on the writing of history, on rhetoric, on political theory, and on strategy.

Lawrence Freedman's *Strategy* questions more deterministic assessments of events in *The History*.[32] Joseph Nye offers a similar warning, questioning not interpretations of Thucydides but Thucydides himself. "It is perhaps imprudent to question Thucydides, the father figure of historians," he begins cautiously, "but very little is every truly inevitable in history... The security dilemma [between Athens and Sparta] made war highly probable, but highly probable is not the same as inevitable,"[33] Both the determinism criticized by Freedman and the inevitability criticized by Nye, however, are based on an imprecise translation of Thucydides, which we will explore in greater detail in chapter 2.

The ease with which we can fall into such traps has prompted many scholars to ride to Thucydides's rescue. Mark Kauppi writing in *Security Studies* urged IR scholars to take a broader look at the theoretical perspectives found in Thucydides.[34] Laurie Johnson-Bagby lamented the "Use and Abuse of Thucydides in International Relations," in a major article from 1994.[35] Ilias Kouskouvelis identified "cherry-picking" as the "the most common phenomena and reasons for the abuse of Thucydides." Such practices, in his view, create "confusion about the text and even about historical reality, and a self-referential way of reading which perpetuates mistakes."[36] David Welch provocatively titled a 2003 article "Why International Relations theorists should stop reading Thucydides," deriding his "largely pernicious" influence on IR theory. Welch's argument, similar to our own, is that those reading Thucydides must:

> stop trying to bend him to our will by making him speak to debates about which he would understand little and care even less. We should stop treating him as a mirror for our own assumptions, convictions, and biases. We should stop competing for his imprimatur. And, perhaps most importantly of all, we should stop trying to reduce his subtle and sophisticated work to a series of simplistic banalities.[37]

One might add, we must also stop using him as a strawman, oversimplifying what he says in order to make it easier for us to discredit his purported views.

Whatever our motivation, these abuses, as Welch explains, are often the result of the "habits of selective reading, misattribution (or at least unjustifiable attribution), the confusion of evidence with authority, and anachronism."[38] Welch presents the interpretation of Thucydides as the father of realism as an example of this abuse through oversimplification. Part of his solution is to "recover our distance from Thucydides."[39] But another component must be to try and divorce ourselves from our moment and to immerse ourselves in Thucydides's world in order to understand the roots of his arguments. The use of Thucydides to tie the past to the present is sadly common in both IR texts and in teaching approaches. For IR scholars and security practitioners alike, the contents of Thucydides's book are constantly tailored to "meet the taste of an immediate public"[40] at the expense of its substance.

Depending on the circumstances of the present and the biases of the author, Thucydides's description of the outbreak of the Peloponnesian War is seen as an analogy to World War I, where alliance blocs drew reluctant powers into a war that no one really wanted or understood.[41] It is a mirror of the Cold War as a "global conflict" in the context of a bipolar system.[42] The Sicilian campaign is analogous to the Vietnam War, where a lack of domestic support under-resourced and betrayed an expeditionary force.[43] If the analogies are to be useful, however, they must be grounded in the accuracy of the empirical data presented in the historical record, not least within the account of Thucydides himself.

The Vietnam example provides a useful opportunity for elaboration. During the 1972–73 academic year, the president of the U.S. Naval War College, Admiral Stansfield Turner, famously added Thucydides to the curriculum. Turner's students, by his own admission, considered it "something of a shock" to study wars that "were nearly twenty-five hundred years ago," but he was convinced of the utility of presenting them with a number of "fundamental considerations," which "have not changed all that much, over the years."[44] So far, so good. Thucydides is an extremely rich case that can be used to elucidate any number of timeless lessons about international affairs, strategy, and domestic politics. But Turner used *The History* selectively to serve the exigencies of the present. For him, *The History's* primary utility was to deliver a lesson on the danger of launching expeditionary forces far from home. In his reading, the Athenian expedition to Sicily became "overextended" and "bogged down" before it was betrayed by "the people of Athens who refused to continue supporting what was going on so far from home." The analogy of this narrative to Vietnam was, in Turner's view, "obvious."[45] This facile use of history illustrates one of the greatest dangers of using Thucydides. Turner's analogy, while "obvious," is essentially misused. The Athenians in Sicily were supported to extraordinary lengths by the home front. The initial expedition was twice as large as the Assembly originally intended. Its goal—unlike the American expedition in Vietnam —was conquest, first of Syracuse, then of Sicily, and then beyond to Italy and even North Africa. Rather than refusing to continue supporting the campaign, the Athenians sent a large body of reinforcements to Sicily and redeployed other troops to prevent enemy reinforcements from bolstering the position of Athens' enemies. When the expedition was finally defeated—thanks largely to the substantial forces sent to Sicily by Athens's enemies within Greece—the people of Athens could hardly believe that their powerful forces had been lost.[46] And through it all, the Athenians had very nearly succeeded. The failure of the expedition had almost nothing to do with a failure of will on the home front. Such nuances, however, escaped Turner in his search for a timely and tidy parallel. We will elaborate further on the Sicilian expedition in chapter 5.

   In spite of the well-intentioned warnings about misusing Thucydides, the abuse continues. The danger remains that anachronism and simplicity will prevail with the objective of supporting comfortable paradigms. This reliance on simple explanations and direct causality ignores the attention Thucydides devotes to domestic politics, psychological factors, political economy, and organizational decision-making. In seeking analogies over rich detail, scholars and their students miss essential elements.

In this book, we aspire to take Thucydides beyond the banalities that now shackle his work with a focus on five lines of argument. They are by no means exhaustive but respond to several common threats in interpretations of his work. We argue that:

1. It is inaccurate to view the Peloponnesian War as one fought between Athens and Sparta in the context of a straightforward bipolar Hellenic world. The Hellenic world was multipolar, not bipolar. State behavior reflects the dynamics of alliances and allegiances within a multipolar structure, allowing weaker states to influence the actions of the stronger. There was no "trap," as modern observers would have us believe, and we can only understand how the power of Athens "compelled" Sparta to fight if we understand the nature of Athenian power and why it would present a threat to Spartan power.

2. In spite of the "system-level" explanations in Thucydides, *The History* places enormous importance on domestic politics and public opinion as drivers for policy. These internal politics, in turn are heavily influenced by the complex psychology and agency of individuals.

3. While Thucydides's focus is state-on-state conflict, he also reports the important role of contending domestic political forces, civil unrest, and even civil wars in shaping and propelling the larger conflict. We must dig into these dynamics to understand the roots and course of conflict.

4. The simple lesson that the powerful can act as they wish is not unambiguously prescriptive in Thucydides. When the powerful act as they wish, they often set upon a path to their destruction.

5. While framed as a single war between Athens and Sparta, Thucydides's war was a much larger conflict. It involved periods of peace as well as war, the realignment of allies, and the entry of neutrals. Like many major wars, its course and conduct were fundamentally influenced by these changes.

These are some of the fundamental lessons that Thucydides can tell us if
we embrace complexity rather than run from it; the greatest value can be
found by carefully reading this rich text. A narrow focus, a distillation, or
an account that places decisive weight on contemporary policy challenges
will shackle Thucydides in anachronistic analogies or unsupportable
simplicity. Even the greatest works need broad historical context (both
before and after the period they describe), cultural awareness, and precise
textual analysis if we are to derive durable lessons. Without those key
guideposts, interpretations of Thucydides will continue to tell us less
about our world and timeless aspects of international politics and more
about the biases and preoccupations of authors and readers. However,
in the chapters to come we hope to address how this failing occurs and
how it can be overcome.

NOTES

1. Thuc. 1.41 (W).
2. Quoted by Pade, *A Handbook on the Reception of Thucydides*, 30
3. Sommerstein and Bayliss, *Oath and State in Ancient Greece*, 213.
4. Thuc. 3.86.
5. Thucydides provides a famous and flattering description of Athenian democracy during this time in the funeral oration of Pericles (2.35–46).
6. de St. Croix, *Origins of the Peloponnesian War*, 90.
7. Ibid., 138.
8. The modern city of Durrës in Albania. It was so small and previously unimportant to the politics of the Hellenic world that Thucydides famously begins his narrative of the events around it by describing its geographical location: "The city of Epidamnus is on the right of the approach to the Ionic Gulf." Thuc. I.24 (W).
9. Thuc. 1.25.
10. Thuc. 1.60 (W).
11. This is speculation based on the name of Thucydides's father Olorus. An uncommon name with Thracian roots, Olorus was the name of the material grandfather of Cimon, making a family connection between Thucydides and Cimon likely.
12. Diodorus, *Library* 11.39.
13. Thuc. 2.65 (W).
14. Ibid., 2.65 (W).
15. Thuc. 5.26.
16. Ibid., 1.22.
17. Ibid., 8.97
18. S. Kennedy, "A Classic Dethroned," 632.
19. Valla quoted by Pade, *A Handbook to the Reception of Thucydides*, 30.
20. Hobbes, *Leviathan*, 13.6.
21. Thuc. 1.75 (W).
22. See for example: Kaufmann, Parker, and Field, *Understanding International Relations* and Viotti and Kauppi, *International Relations Theory*.
23. Dunne, Kurki, and Smith, *International Relations Theories*, 60.
24. Art and Jervis, *International Politics* (2005), 10.
25. Dougherty and Pfaltzgraff, *Contending Theories of International Relations* (1990), 186.

26. Ibid., 469.

27. Waltz, *Man the State and War*, 216

28. Waltz, *Theory of International Politics*, 66, 186.

29. Mearsheimer, *The Tragedy of Great Power Politics*, 163.

30. Ibid., 365.

31. Caldwell and Williams, *Seeking Security in an Insecure World* (2012), 219.

32. Freedman, *Strategy*, 30–41.

33. Nye, *Understanding International Conflict*, 19.

34. Kauppi, "Thucydides."

35. Johnson-Bagby, "The Use and Abuse of Thucydides."

36. Kouskouvelis, *Thucydides on Choice and Decision Making*, 61.

37. Welch, "Why International Relations Theorists Should Stop Reading Thucydides," 302.

38. Ibid.

39. Ibid., 317.

40. Thuc. 1.22 (W).

41. Dougherty and Pfaltzcraff, *Contending Theories of International Relations*.

42. Forde, "Thucydides on Peace," 40.

43. Turner, "Address to Chicago Council Navy League."

44. Ibid.

45. Ibid.

46. Thuc. 8.1.

CHAPTER 2

THE POLARITY TRAP

SYSTEMIC ERRORS AND THINKING THROUGH CHOICE

"What made war inevitable was the growth of Athenian power and the fear this caused in Sparta."[1]

—Thucydides

"The Thucydides Paradox is the way that all the authority of a complex, ambiguous author is used to legitimise [sic] a simplistic, reductionist account of his work."[2]

—Neville Morley

Ever since Thucydides penned his famous line that what made war necessary for the Spartans was the growth of Athenian power and the fear this caused in Sparta, students of international relations have been forced to confront the "systemic" causes of war. According to this interpretation of international politics, wars occur not so much due to choice, intent, or policy but because of underlying characteristics within the international system. Depending on one's translation, Thucydides writes that the Spartans were "compelled" to go to war or that their fear made it "necessary" for them to go to war. As with several passages in Thucydides, there is a rich historical and philological debate on this subject, which we do not need to deal with directly here. In the present context, it is sufficient to observe that the canonical interpretation argues that systemic factors drove the two rivals to war; this factor made war "inevitable."[3] Michael Howard chooses the Warner translation of "inevitable" war.[4] Paul Rahe also comments on the inevitability of conflict, noting the characteristics and differences of Sparta and Athens, and observes that "[i]t was perhaps inevitable that two such polities came to blows."[5] Kenneth Waltz cites the more ominous (and accurate, in this case) 1900 Jowett version, which asserts that the growth of Athenian power meant that Sparta was "forced" into war.[6] Thucydides uses the word *anagkasai*, which means that the Spartans were "compelled" or "forced" to make war. The forcing mechanism, at least according to the sentence in question, is what Thucydides describes as "the growth of Athenian power." There is a more detailed analysis of this subject through the lenses of power and fear in chapter 3.

This systemic explanation is frequently described as one of Thucydides's most prominent contributions to international relations theory. It is a simple premise, which underpins structural realist interpretations of geopolitics. Changes in the distribution of power within the system lead to war as a rising power threatens to overthrow an established hegemon. The potentially explosive dynamics of this relationship is the essence of Thucydides's Trap as explained by Allison.[7] This phenomenon is essentially the same as Robert Gilpin's theory of "hegemonic transition."[8] This structural interpretation, however, is grounded on an imprecise translation of Thucydides. More importantly, it is an oversimplification of the dynamics he presents in the rest of his work and of other elements we can analyze within the historical record.

This chapter will unpack this theoretical law attributed to Thucydides. It will demonstrate that, in spite of widely held opinion, Thucydides does not explain the conflict between Athens and Sparta primarily in structural terms but through decisions taken by major powers to preserve security alliances, by the realignment of neutrals, and by the actions of allies whose interests were directly under threat. Thucydides emphasizes choice, debate, and individual agency rather than inevitability. These developments occurred within the context of a multipolar, rather than a bipolar, system. Thucydides paints a picture of the failure of deterrence and also of the mistaken assumptions on the part of leaders. These decisions are not the function of systemic imperatives but are deeply rooted in domestic politics, including the personality, preferences, and persuasiveness of policymakers, all of which go beyond explanations based on factors at the "systemic" level. These principles have proven their value in explaining not only the conflict between Athens and Sparta but also other cases of great power war. They explain not only why Athens and Sparta went to war but also, critically, why they went to war when they did. They provide not only the necessary causes but also the sufficient ones.

We will begin with an exploration of two assumptions implicit in the analysis of hegemonic transition—Spartan hegemony and systemic bipolarity. These assumptions are problematic and require additional explanation. Our argument pursues three lines of analysis: that Sparta was not a hegemonic power, that its nature (and the dynamics of Hellenic politics during this period) prevented it from being one, and that the international system in which Athens and Sparta functioned was multi-polar rather than bipolar. Whereas this chapter will engage in some analysis of the nature of the distribution of power within the system, largely to demonstrate the critical reliance Sparta had on its allies, in the next chapter we will attempt to develop a more nuanced conception of power in line with the evidence offered by Thucydides and history

This chapter will next address how individual actors and deci-sion-makers shaped policy choices. Thucydides devotes a great deal of effort expounding on the role of debate, individual agency, and choice. This approach contradicts the view that he is convinced of the inevitability of structural factors in leading nations to war. Furthermore, the essen-tially competitive nature of domestic politics in both Athens and Sparta (particularly in the former) meant that no decision was "inevitable." Part of the fundamental richness of Thucydides's account is to present the agency of leaders in domestic politics and the influence of individual leaders on events. These factors also undermine systemic explanations. They force us to confront the significant impact of individuals and the influence of debates in the context of domestic politics in decisions about war and peace.

AN INEVITABLE ERROR

An argument focusing on structural stress within the international system rests on two key assumptions drawn from a single sentence in Thucydides's *The History*, that "what made war inevitable was the growth of Athenian power and the fear which this caused in Sparta."[9] IR theorists often derive two assumptions about the system from this sentence: systemic bipolarity and Spartan hegemony. Both can only be implicit in Thucydides's formulation; nevertheless, they have become canonical. If we go beyond that sentence, however, we see that through the rest of his book, Thucydides does not paint a picture that defends this interpretation. Instead, he creates the picture of a multipolar world in which power was difficult to measure. Spartan hegemony was a chimera. There was a rudimentary international system of competing states, but the rules of this order were neither defined nor supported in any meaningful way by Sparta. Sparta was extremely powerful, but it was not in any sense hegemonic. Its demographics and system of government were just two obstacles to achieving or exercising anything approaching hegemony. Because of the fundamental difficulties in measuring power, the relationship between Sparta and Athens was so ambiguous and difficult to define that even Thucydides is contradictory about whether Sparta or Athens was the superior power.[10] He portrays the Spartans themselves as agnostic about which state was more powerful.[11] As we will show, the discourse of hegemonic transition confronts similar problems and results in similar confusion. We will begin by analyzing the claim of systemic bipolarity.

On its face, it might seem that Spartan hegemony and systemic bipolarity are incompatible. If Sparta were a hegemonial power, then this suggests that the system itself would be unipolar. If the system were bipolar, then neither Sparta nor any other power could be considered a hegemon. For the concept of Thucydides's Trap to work, the international system where it plays out must be bipolar. Gilpin, who pioneered the theory of hegemonic war, describes a process by which hegemony (unipolarity) becomes bipolarity. He ascribes tension to that process itself. Initially, the system is dominated by the hegemon. This hegemon sees its power eroding as the subordinate state "begins to grow disproportionately... The ensuing struggle between these two states and their respective allies leads to a bipolarization of the system, to an inevitable crisis, and eventually to a hegemonic war."[12] Hegemony is therefore replaced by bipolarity, which, in turn, leads to war.

Thucydides's account of a rising Athens challenging hegemonic Sparta is the bedrock on which this analysis rests. This is a splintered and unstable foundation upon which to build. Thucydides's world was a multipolar one. Moreover, as we will argue in the next chapter, it was also a world (much like our own) where power was multifaceted and not easy to quantify or define in concrete terms. The implications of a multipolar world are significant. Without bipolarity, the struggle between Athens and Sparta cannot be framed as a hegemonic war. It was not brought about by systemic level forces as Thucydides's Trap would have us believe. Instead, we must look to the actions taken by Spartan and Athenian policymakers as well as the policies employed by other actors in the system. Outside of a bipolar framework, the choices and interests of important neutrals, like Corcyra, and critical Spartan allies, like Corinth, were essential in the road to war. Once the war began, the actions of other major powers like Persia, Thebes, Argos, and Syracuse had a decisive impact on the struggle's course.

"The war broke out," writes Donald Kagan, "in a particular international structure that political scientists call 'bipolar,' and theorists believe that structure helps explain the coming of wars."[13] For Kagan, a classical historian, bipolarity is a moniker cribbed from a foreign discipline. As such, it is promptly attacked. Such general theories, in Kagan's view, are "not very satisfying" because they only explain conditions under which war becomes likely. "[T]hey do not explain why particular wars come about."[14] One might add that a systemic factor like bipolarity can establish underlying conditions that might increase the likelihood of conflict without telling us anything about why that conflict breaks out at a particular time. In other words, they may be necessary, but they are not sufficient. Kagan's point is a valid one and grows in importance as we consider the Hellenic world in greater depth.

War was a near constant feature of the ancient Greek world. War between Sparta and Athens was no exception to this rule. After the Persian invasions of Greece (490–478 BCE), the Spartans and Athenians fought no fewer than three wars against each other. Sparta and Athens fought each other during the First Peloponnesian War (460 and 445), the "great" Peloponnesian War (431–404) that is the subject of *The History*, and the Corinthian War (395–387). Any student wishing to derive lessons from the war must grapple with this historical context. Extending our view both before and after Thucydides's war alters the nature of our question. It is not why Athens and Sparta fought; it is why they fought a particular war beginning in 431 and why they fought it in the manner that they did.

Kagan appears to raise the issue of bipolarity in relation to the Peloponnesian War only to dismiss its utility, but others, particularly political scientists, have not followed this example. Thucydides remains an important data point for subsequent theories grounded in bipolarity in spite of the fact that the bipolar character of fifth century Greece is debatable. Bipolarity has been challenged but not in a systemic way.[15] It remains the easy consensus among political scientists seeking to derive lessons from Thucydides. Raymond Aron,[16] Peter Fleiss,[17] Steven Forde,[18] Carlo Santoro,[19] Robert Gilpin,[20] John Mearsheimer,[21] and Athanasios

Platias and Constantinos Koliopoulos,[22] among many others, argue that bipolarity defined the Athenian-Spartan world. According to this line of argument, bipolarity also determined the behavior of the various actors. Moreover, bipolarity as a systemic condition has predictive power across time. Gilpin is convinced that the "bipolar structure" of "fifth century Greece... created the necessary conditions for war,"[23] and goes so far as to describe conflict in bipolar systems as practically inescapable.[24] There is neither mystery nor agency in describing the coming of the conflict. It is, by Gilpin's own assessment (supported by the erroneous translation of Thucydides), "inevitable."

Even agnostics who hedge against this fatalistic view acknowledge that bipolar systems are characterized by heightened tension and are "more seriously threatened by a generalized and inexorable war."[25] This reliance on explanations grounded in the system's polarity demands a critical analysis of the actual distribution of power. This is possible only through a rigorous approach to the available historical data combined with a theoretical foundation that adequately defines bipolarity.

In spite of the term's frequent use, the definition of bipolarity is neither clear nor universal.[26] In 1964, Kenneth Waltz described it as a system where two powers each possessed "global interests which it can care for unaided."[27] Waltz resisted describing bipolarity in stronger terms, writing that it would "misinterpret the history of the post-war world."[28] In his concept, bipolarity is simply a condition in which "there is a great gap between the power of the two leading countries and the power of the next most considerable states."[29] Waltz's comment about the post-war world is significant, since it was the dynamics created by the Cold War that necessitated a concept like bipolarity. For the rest of world history, international politics had centered on the complications posed by multipolarity, great power competition, and shifting alliances.

Wagner's later observation that there was no adequate definition for bipolarity was telling. A fixation on bipolarity in the context of 1993 was ironic because the "bipolarity" that defined the Cold War had already ended. Nevertheless, it was the Cold War that had made the term "bipolarity" necessary. Its end thrust the world into the *terra incognita* of unipolarity but carried the latent threat of the instability of a multipolar world familiar from the conflict-laden first half of the twentieth century.

In *Ways of War and Peace*, Michael Doyle hedges his bets in defining the polarity of the system by attempting to create a more nuanced description of the Hellenic world than the traditional one of bipolarity. He describes the structure of the system in the 430s BCE as quasi-bipolar. Two alliance blocs did exist, but the "composition of power" within them "was not identical."[30] In a quasi-bipolar world

> some of the logic of multipolar politics applied... Neither Athens nor Sparta could be indifferent [to their allies], they were not superior enough. In a multipolar system, on the other hand, alliances shift to reflect multiple changes in relative power. But Athens and Sparta were each too large to be readily balanced by marginal shifts in alliances.[31]

Doyle is correct that the system had features of multi-polarity. Sparta, in particular, could not be "indifferent" to its allies. In fact, we see that it was precisely a need to keep allies content with the structure of the Peloponnesian League that was a major factor in Sparta's decision to go to war. But to characterize the position of Corcyra, the alignment of Corinth, or the intervention of Persia as a "marginal shift" is to misunderstand the relative power dynamics of the Greek world at the time. All were significant powers in their own right.

Corcyra's alignment—due to its possession of the third-largest naval force in the Hellenic world—was key to the balance of forces at sea, which the Athenians recognized. Corinth's departure from the Spartan alliance would not have constituted a "marginal" shift in alliances. Such a course of action would have isolated Sparta in the Peloponnese and posed significant security implications, which we will address presently. Geographically, an alliance with Corinth was the best balance against Argos, Sparta's traditional enemy just to its north and a foreign-policy imperative for Sparta.[32] Corinth's defection would also leave Sparta deficient in naval resources. Corinth manned the second-largest navy in the Hellenic world. Persia, on its own merits, was large enough to fight both Sparta and Athens combined, as it had done during the first half of the fifth century. It was another great power very much within the system.

Doyle's error seems partially explained by inaccuracies in his empirical evidence. For example, he quotes an accurate figure for Athenian hoplites (the heavy infantry, normally drawn from those citizens who could afford the cost of purchasing their own armor and weapons)—twenty-nine thousand[33]—but places the number of Spartan hoplites at fifty thousand— an impossibly large figure, almost twice the manpower of Athens.[34] Historians studying Sparta during this period, place their manpower in the region of between three thousand five hundred and four thousand.[35] Doyle's number is more than fourteen times larger than such estimates. Such a figure is only possible if it includes forces from all of Sparta's dependent helots, clients, and allies.[36] Sparta could call upon some of these resources in exceptional circumstances. Its reliance on such measures to effectively match Athenian strength shows the lack of true systemic bipolarity. The wild divergence between Sparta's strength according to Doyle and its actual strength exposes the basic empirical errors at the root of several explanations of bipolarity.

In "What was bipolarity?" R. Harrison Wagner explores different concepts of bipolarity, writing that the term has "four distinct meanings." For Wagner, the possible meanings of bipolarity are:

1) a condition in which states are polarized into two hostile coalitions
2) a condition in which there are only two states capable of a strategy of global deterrence;
3) a system of only two states; and

4) a system in which power is distributed in such a way that two states are so powerful that they can defend themselves against any combination of other states.[37]

Wagner's construction finds direction from Waltz's description of bipolarity. Like Waltz, Wagner consciously admits his definitions were developed in the context of the Cold War.

But can any of Wagner's four categories be applied to the Eastern Mediterranean in the fifth century BCE? Definition three is clearly not applicable. There were more than two states in the system. As Wagner admits, a system with only two states has never occurred.[38] Definition four, in which two states are so powerful that they can defend themselves against any combination of other states, is clearly not applicable either. Defending itself against any combination of other states was precisely what Athens was not able to do. It was the combination of the power of Sparta and its allies, the defection of allies within its own empire, and Persian intervention that defeated Athens. The second definition, although enmeshed in twentieth century politics and technological developments, raises the questions of deterrence and the projection of power. No state from the fifth century BCE exercised global power. War was frequent; deterrence was rare. Moreover, as a term, "deterrence" and its utility are now frequently bound up in modern analyses of the role of nuclear weapons.

During the fifth century BCE, at least four powers—Persia, Athens, Sparta, and Corinth—were capable of projecting power within their effective world. The Persian Empire was the equal of either Athens or Sparta. In terms of the land mass and population under its control, it was far superior to both combined. During the war, both Athens and Sparta sought Persian aid. Sparta was victorious, in the end, largely because it secured a Persian alliance. Since it is a gross historical inaccuracy to classify the world as bipolar if Persia is included, some scholars circumvent the problem by referring to bipolarity solely within "the system of the Greek city-states."[39] But even within a purely Greek context, there were other major powers. We have already touched on Corinth, but, in addition, we must consider influential neutral states like Argos and Syracuse. A historical Spartan foe, Argos remained neutral at the start of the Peloponnesian War. It had a powerful army and a large territorial base. Syracuse controlled the second-largest physical territory of any *polis* in the Greek world after Sparta; it was neutral at the start of the war. As Thucydides himself points out and as the Athenian defeat in its expedition of 415–413 confirmed, Syracuse was a major power in its own right.[40]

This leaves us with having to test the validity of Wagner's first definition of bipolarity: a system "polarized into two hostile coalitions," exacerbated by a lack of "cleavages cutting across the line dividing the two blocs" and without the possibility of "shifting alliances to redress imbalances of power between coalitions."[41] In the *Theory of International Politics*, Waltz makes an important distinction between "the formation of two blocs in a multipolar world and... structural bipolarity."[42] It was precisely a system of two blocs within a multi-polar world, rather than structural bipolarity, that characterized the Greek world of the fifth century. There were two hostile, or at least potentially hostile, coalitions. What about cleavages and shifts in alliances?

Defining bipolarity in terms of "two hostile coalitions" attempts to forge a somewhat unsatisfactory compromise. It acknowledges that there are more than two powers that matter, but then constrains them within their respective coalitions thereby denying their agency. Eckstein attempts to defend this construction of hostile coalitions by arguing that although the Hellenic world in 470 was "in essence divided between allies of Athens and allies of Sparta [and characterized by] a condition of bitter rivalrous bipolarity," the "fundamental bipolarity was complicated by the fact that powerful states such as Corcyra, Argos, and Corinth were well able to play independent (often destructive) roles within the system."[43]

Understanding the independence and importance of actors beyond the two major powers is precisely the issue. Wagner's "cleavages" are defined as largely ideological impediments to communication and compromise. These were certainly greater in the Cold War case than in the case presented by Thucydides. While some have argued about the ethnic-linguistic division between the Ionian Athenians and the Dorian Spartans, both *poleis* shared a common Greek culture. They conversed in essentially the same language, worshipped the same gods, shared holy sites and religious rites, and participated in the Olympic Games along with the other city-states of the Greek world.

While they practiced apparently different forms of government, Athenian direct democracy and Sparta's circumscribed constitutional monarchy nevertheless had a great deal in common. The two systems certainly had more in common, for example, than American republicanism and Soviet communism (or communism's present Chinese incarnation). Modern interpretations of a fundamental ideological cleavage between Athens and Sparta are accurate only to a point. These arguments, epitomized by Hanson, emphasize the threat Athens posed to Sparta with its "radical ideology" at once "proselytizing and expansionary."[44] But Hanson's argument owes too much to the contemporary discourse of "democracy promotion." It is, at its heart, anachronistic. Both Athens and Sparta were slave states.[45] Both jealously guarded their citizenship and political freedom. Both had assemblies of those male citizens to vote on key legislative issues and foreign policies. Both employed political systems that provided functional advantages to eminent families whose influence was based on wealth and lineage. Both used war as a tool of policy. Neither was shy of committing acts of brutality. Both were committed to the belief that their system represented the most functional mix of political freedom, order, and justice. Both states engaged in formal diplomacy, entered into formal alliances, treaty constructions, and adhered to a set of (admittedly rugged and nascent) international norms.

The most salient point about the rigid division between the two blocs, however, is Wagner's view on the inflexibility of alliances within a bipolar system. Between Athens and Sparta, as Thucydides's story clearly demonstrates, it was the shifting of alliances that was a fundamental root of the conflict. As Waltz argues, in a multipolar system there is a high degree of military interdependence among allies: "[g]reat powers in a multipolar world depend on one another for political and military support in crises and war... in a bipolar world... third parties are not able to tilt the balance of power by withdrawing from one alliance or by joining the other."[46] It was precisely this ability to "tilt the balance"—characteristic of multipolar system dynamics—that drew Athens into alliance with Corcyra in the first place. The essence of the Corcyraean argument to Athens was that if Athens failed to accept Corcyra as an ally, Corcyra would be conquered by Corinth. Through conquest, Corinth would add the strength of Corcyra to its navy, which already was the second-largest navy in the Greek world. This would shift the balance of forces at sea away from Athens and in favor of Corinth and, through Corinth, to Sparta.[47] Spartan leaders openly acknowledged that to defeat Athens they would have to call up the resources of their existing allies and win over new ones "from any quarter."[48] This was undoubtedly a veiled reference to the need for Persian support—another hitherto neutral third party capable of tilting the balance of power.

Corinth itself provides a powerful example of the potential for cleavages and realignments within the two alliance blocs. During the debate in Sparta to determine whether Athens violated the Thirty Years Peace, Corinth makes an open threat to the Spartan assembly. "Give your allies... the help you promised," urged the Corinthian envoys. "Do not force the rest of us in despair to join a different alliance."[49] We can infer that this threat of realignment, of Corinth away from Sparta, was credible based on subsequent events. In 421, ten years into the Peloponnesian War, the Spartans agreed to the Peace of Nicias and a treaty of fifty years with the Athenians. At the assembly of the Peloponnesian League, Corinth voted against this peace agreement and then refused to be bound by its terms.[50] Corinth then made good on its threat to join a different alliance by allying with Argos against Sparta.[51]

An analysis of the power of Corinth in conjunction with an analysis of the relationship of Corinthian power to Sparta exposes the fallacy of bipolarity within the Greek world. Corinth possessed the second-largest navy in Hellas, a significant economy, and its own web of colonies. It had foreign policy goals that were distinct from those of Sparta, and, as evident in the case of Corcyra, it would wage war without Sparta. This independent foreign policy, coupled with Corinth's power and the influence it exerted as Sparta's ally, proved critical in the origins and course of the Great Peloponnesian War. And it is precisely the nature of Sparta's relationship with allies like Corinth that contradicts the claim of Spartan hegemony.

THE HOLLOW HEGEMON

Both hegemonic transition theory and Thucydides's Trap depend on a dynamic where an established hegemon is challenged by a rising power. In most interpretations of Thucydides, the respective roles are played by Sparta and Athens.[52] But Thucydides's *The History* and the weight of other historical evidence suggest a different picture. Not only was the Hellenic world multipolar rather than bipolar, Sparta was far from being a hegemon within it. Spartan power was intimately linked with its diplomatic construction, the Peloponnesian League. This association was neither a Spartan empire nor a unitary coalition. Instead, it was "a loose organization consisting of Sparta, on the one hand, and a group of allies connected to her by separate treaties on the other."[53] These bilateral treaties reflected the distinctive nature of the various Spartan clients. Kagan identifies three categories of Spartan allies:

> states that were small enough and close enough to Sparta as to be easily controlled... [states which] were stronger, more remote, or both, but not so powerful and distant as to escape ultimate punishment... [and] states so far removed and mighty in their own

right that their conduct of foreign policy was rarely subordinated to Spartan interests.

Only Thebes and Corinth were in this final category.[54]

The nature of these relationships contradicts a "hegemonic" inter-pretation of Spartan power. As a hegemon, Sparta would have been expected to control and dominate "the lesser states in the system." As part of a bipolar structure, it would have regulated "interactions within and between [its sphere] of influence."[55] But Sparta did not regulate interactions within the broader system. Its hegemony was based on military leadership and its strength as a land power. In other realms, it made few pretenses to leadership or control. Its economy was agrarian in nature, and Spartans eschewed trade. The Spartans had no public treasury for funds and did not even produce their own coins until after the Peloponnesian War. They were wary of foreigners and of having their own citizens travel to foreign lands, even when on military campaign. Ideologically, Spartans were afraid of corruption through dealing with the outside world. As one modern historian has put it, they "thought of themselves quite literally as a breed apart."[56] These factors placed real limits on any purported Spartan hegemony.

If they conformed to the Spartan ideal, Spartan leaders were too conservative and inward looking to lead a pan-Hellenic alliance. If they abandoned the Spartan ideal—as many who came into contact with the outside world did—greed, arrogance, and self-aggrandizing tendencies usually spelled their downfall. In 478, for example, following the defeat of the Persians at the battle of Plataea, Greek allies were unwilling to accept Spartan leadership because of the corrupt and high-handed manner of their leading commanders.[57] This opposition, combined with the near betrayal of the Spartan general Pausanias to Persia, convinced the Spartans that "they no longer wanted to be burdened with the war against Persia."[58] In a manner very unlike a hegemon, they surrendered the leadership of the Hellenic coalition to the Athenians and so paved the way for the creation of the Delian League and the Athenian Empire.

If we look beyond Thucydides, we also find evidence that shows the limitations of Spartan power. With Athens defeated at the conclusion of the Peloponnesian War, the record suggests that Sparta did indeed launch a bid for hegemony within the Hellenic world. After the defeat of Athens, Sparta led the overthrow of democratic regimes and their replacement with friendly oligarchies. It deployed *harmosts* (military governors) in reluctant allies and garrisons in order to retain control. The result was an almost immediate and wide-ranging rebellion against Spartan interests. Erstwhile allies like Corinth and Thebes banded with former enemies like Athens and Persian in a grand anti-Spartan coalition that soon brought Spartan power to the breaking point. In less than a decade, Sparta squandered the fruits of its victory, and the tenuous basis for its hegemonial bid was cruelly exposed. These events will be dealt with in greater detail in chapter 6.

Sparta's apparent inability to lead was not simply a matter of character. Spartan elites were also aware of the fundamental physical limitations of their state. Although Sparta was a major power, it could not compete with Athens in demographic terms. There are two arguments to be made here and, fortunately, we do not need to choose between them since both result in fewer full Spartan citizens, *homoioi* (peers).[59] In one interpretation, there were fewer Spartans because their system conspired to keep the population artificially low in real terms. Numbers are always hard to come by when studying the ancient world, but, according to the first argument, several societal factors meant that there were few Spartans despite the size of Sparta's domains and their agricultural fertility. These social practices, when combined with the fact that the Spartan state was nearly continuously at war, resulted in manpower shortages.

The second argument ascribes Sparta's manpower shortage not to the absence of people *per se* but to the absence of Spartan citizens proper. In other words, there were not fewer people in Sparta, just fewer male children of Spartan parents sufficiently well off to afford the requirements of citizenship, particularly the fees at the communal mess-halls, and qualify as Spartiate *homoioi*. In this interpretation, put forward by Aristotle (and later favored by Marxist historians), it was the tendency of Spartans to have large families that reduced the land allotments available through primogenitor and drove many Spartans below the wealth threshold for full citizenship.[60] This would not have reduced the size of Spartan armies *per se*. Instead, it would have reduced the number of elite *homoioi* within those armies. As the number of *homoioi* declined, so too did the effectiveness and capability of Sparta's armies.

Regardless of the underlying causes, the historical record shows a clear decline in the number of Spartan *homoioi*. One modern exegesis has neatly laid out the inexorable decline in Spartan manpower in support of Aristotle's basic claim of oliganthropy—a shortage of citizens: eight thousand full citizen hoplites in 480, three thousand five hundred in 418, two thousand five hundred in 394, and finally only one thousand five hundred men identified as Spartan "peers" in 371.[61] These are hardly demographics capable of sustaining hegemony.

Because the number of full Spartan citizens was always relatively low, Spartan power projection was dependent on the unique training of its limited forces and the substantial numerical support of its allies. A quantitative analysis of the number of troops involved in Sparta's major battles during the fifth century reinforces the hypothesis that Sparta depended on its allies to wage war, even on land and even at the height of its power. A clear pattern is discernible in the historical record of Sparta deploying *homoioi* as "shock troops" within larger forces. At the legendary defense of Thermopylae in 480, three hundred Spartans were the strike force of an army that totaled between four thousand and seven thousand hoplites. A year later, five thousand Spartans—the largest recorded Spartan force—spearheaded a combined army of nearly forty thousand Greek hoplites that defeated the Persians at Plataea.[62] At the battle of Tanagra in 457, only one thousand five hundred Spartans took the field supported by ten thousand allies against the "entire army" of Athens—some thirteen thousand hoplites—and one thousand

Argives.[63] At the first Battle of Mantinea—the largest pitched battle of the Great Peloponnesian War—Thucydides estimates that there were three thousand five hundred Spartans within an army of nine thousand against eight thousand Argives, Athenians, and their allies. He also adds that because of the "secrecy with which their affairs are conducted... no one knew the numbers of Spartans."[64] By 394, only two thousand five hundred men qualified as peers. By 371, the number was down to one thousand five hundred.[65] Such numbers make it clear that, on its own, Sparta could not hope to sustain a position as hegemon. By the numbers, it could not even sustain an army large enough to wage war against any of the major powers of the Hellenic world.

If Sparta relied on allies to fight on land, it had even more transparent need for allies at sea. Athens, Thucydides relates, had three hundred warships ready for action at the start of the Peloponnesian War, which represented the largest single naval power in the Greek world.[66] In comparison, Corcyra, the third-largest naval power, had a fleet of a least one hundred and twenty ships.[67] We also know from Thucydides that Corinth possessed the second-largest navy in the Greek world, putting its number of ships somewhere above the one hundred and twenty ships of Corcyra and below the three hundred ships of Athens. In the clash between Corcyraean and Corinthian forces off the Sybota islands, Corinth deployed ninety ships within a contingent of one hundred and fifty.[68] In contrast, the naval resources of Sparta and her allies are estimated by Kagan to have been in the region of one hundred ships.[69] As further context, the Persian Empire committed approximately two hundred ships against the Greek coalition at the battle of Eurymedon in 466.[70]

In any confrontation with Athens, Sparta needed the Corinthian fleet and, to take the offensive, support from Persia as well. Thucydides claims that when the war broke out, the Spartans planned a massive building program, working with its allies as far away as Italy to raise the five hundred ships they thought necessary to oppose Athens.[71] In the early stages of the war, knowing that it lacked the manpower and economic resources to build a fleet of sufficient size to take the war at sea to Athens, Sparta also began attempts to conclude an anti-Athenian alliance with Persia to supply the ships that they needed.[72] According to Sparta's plan, its allies were meant to supply fully more than four-fifths of their side's naval power.

These empirical realities paint the picture of a Sparta that was dependent on its allies for major military campaigns.[73] We can call upon geography to further support this argument of dependency. Sparta's operational plan for war with Athens involved the invasion of the Athenian homeland in Attica. As Sparta did not have command of the sea, this invasion would have to come overland, across the Isthmus of Corinth and then through mountainous terrain east towards Attica and Athens. Such an invasion, it was hoped, would destroy Athenian resources, farms, homesteads, and agricultural production. It would break the will of the Athenian *demos* and push it towards peace. The Athenian army would either come out to fight and be defeated by Sparta's superior land forces or would hole up in Athens for a siege. Here the problem in Sparta's campaign plan began to show. The Spartans lacked the resources to take Athens by storm. Nor were they able to keep sufficient forces deployed for a siege because they were vulnerable on the home front to a helot insurrection. Deploying the bulk of Sparta's forces north in an invasion also left the home front vulnerable to an Athenian counterattack. Athens might (and did) sail an invasion force of their own to the Peloponnese with the express purpose of undermining Spartan control of the peninsula and spurring the helots to revolt.[74] It was precisely the implementation of this tactic that brought the Spartan army home to the Peloponnese after only a 15-day stay in Attica in the campaigning season of 425.[75]

To get to Attica, Sparta had to march its forces almost the entire length of the Peloponnese. These forces had to cross the Isthmus of Corinth—controlled, naturally enough, by Corinth. The loss of Corinthian support would leave Spartan forces bottled up in the Peloponnese where they would be unable to threaten Athens in any meaningful way. Once across the isthmus, Spartan forces then had to navigate their way around several mountain ranges towards Athens, leaving those forces with few potential routes. The most plausible of these was through the Megarid —heightening the importance of maintaining an alliance with Megara. During the First Peloponnesian War (460–445), Athens had succeeded in winning over Megara and blocking the progress of Spartan forces through the Megarid and so avoided invasion. At Tanagra, it forced a large Spartan army to give battle and risk the disastrous implications of a defeat far from home with its escape route and supply lines under threat. The Spartans won the day and were then able to withdraw to the Peloponnese overland, "devastating the Megarid in passing."[76]

Thucydides offers us an invaluable window into the critical need Sparta had for allied support in its military campaigns through his account of the conduct of their foreign policy. At the outbreak of the Great Peloponnesian War, after the Spartan assembly voted that Athens had violated the terms of their peace treaty, they did not immediately launch an invasion. Instead

> [t]hey then summoned their allies to the assembly and told them that they had decided that Athens was acting aggressively, but that they wanted to have all their allies with them when they put the vote, so that, if they decided to make war, it should be done on the basis of a unanimous resolution.[77]

Here, Thucydides is hinting at the way Sparta's Peloponnesian League functioned. The key structural elements were as follows. As the central power of the league, Sparta, and Sparta alone, could call a league congress. Sparta would routinely first call its own assembly (as Thucydides describes) where Spartan citizens would vote on a particular issue before summoning a congress. The allies would then come to the congress and debate the issue proposed by the Spartans (knowing already how the Spartans had voted). Those allies would then vote on the issue as individual *poleis*. A majority decision "bound all allies, even those who had voted against it."[78] It was only if the majority of allies went against

Sparta's will that no action would be taken. In spite of these conditions, unanimity, or at least a clear majority, was important because Sparta could not make a major foreign policy decision like waging war against Athens without allied support.[79] Even the bellicose Corinthians acknowledged this reality in their speech to the allied congress.[80]

After the debate at the congress closed, Sparta "put the vote city by city to all their allies who were present, both great and small. The majority voted for war."[81] It was not the unanimous decision Sparta had wanted, but it was enough. There was still much to be done before Sparta considered the league ready for a clash of arms. Almost an entire year was spent on preparations and "necessary preliminaries," before Attica could be invaded.[82] Even so, the war did not begin with Spartan forces marching off on an invasion of Athenian territory. Instead, the war began with a secret attack by Thebes, one of Sparta's most power allies, against Plataea, an Athenian client.[83]

Historical evidence both within and beyond Thucydides is clear in refuting both systemic bipolarity and Spartan hegemony. This evidence also supports various theoretical claims about the military dependence and political dependence within multipolar alliances. Shifts in alliance dynamics and the potential for shifts in alignments themselves were critical in generating tensions and played a major role in the outbreak of war. Such shifts would be impossible or irrelevant in a bipolar system. In the multipolar Hellenic world, they proved decisive factors in decisions about war and peace.

In fact, the dynamics of Spartan-Corinthian relations have characteristics of entrapment as defined by Glenn Snyder in "The Security Dilemma in Alliance Politics." Entrapment, Snyder argues, "means being dragged into a conflict over an ally's interests that one does not share, or shares only partially."[84] It was in Corinth's interest rather than that of Sparta to support Epidamnus against Corcyra and prevent the expansion of Corcyraean power in the Adriatic. It was in Corinth's interest first to harness the specter of Spartan support to prevent Athens from supporting

Corcyra and then to prevent the Athenian conquest of Corinth's colony at Potidaea. Corinth needed Spartan support in its confrontation with Athens and threatened to leave its alliance with Sparta if this support was not forthcoming. When Sparta adopted a policy of conciliation with Athens in 421, Corinth did, in fact, abandon its alliance with Sparta, albeit briefly.

Entrapment is possible, Snyder argues, "when one values the preservation of the alliance more than the cost of fighting for the ally's interests."[85] In this interpretation, Sparta was willing to demonstrate its commitment to its Corinthian ally through a limited exercise of force against Athens. Sparta feared losing Corinth as an ally more than it feared a military confrontation with Athens and more than it feared the growth of Athenian power, *per se*. It would, perhaps, be more accurate to say that Sparta feared the defection of Corinth from its alliance in the event Sparta failed to show sufficient resolve in backing Corinth against Athens. Such a defection was only plausible and substantial under the prevailing conditions of multipolarity. This is a less elegant, but more precise, explanation for Sparta's behavior and gives a more accurate sort of "trap" confronting policymakers than shorthands of Thucydides 1.23. These policymakers too, have their role in Thucydides's account. Their influence in shaping domestic politics and the role of domestic politics itself is prominent in *The History* and provides further evidence to repudiate systemic explanations. Whereas the factor of domestic politics will be an essential element of our analysis in chapter 4, we may proceed here with a brief analysis of choice in Thucydides.

Choice

Any emphasis on the system as the driving force behind Thucydides's story also founders on the degree to which *The History* is devoted to individual actors and their choices. Many IR scholars privilege the presumed structural causes of the war and, as a result, diminish the impact of domestic politics and choice. This interpretation argues that:

all the political and constitutional differences in terms of empire or hegemony between the two opposed subsystems, in both ancient and modern bipolarity are important, but in the long run not decisive. The role of domestic political system can certainly influence the way in which the systemic rules are functioning, but cannot reverse them.[86]

Such an argument is not confirmed by Thucydides's approach or by the course of events. Through speeches and debates, Thucydides presents a window into the internal politics of various actors, especially Athens and Sparta, to explain why they behaved the way they did. While some of his statements affirm a structural condition that influenced the outbreak of the war, he does not explain the war in such terms alone. Critically, Thucydides is also interested in "human nature."[87] Human nature creates behaviors that are both rational and irrational. Rationality itself, as historians know, is not always universal in its perception. Influenced by history, personal ambition, and national culture, decision-making in Thucydides is "anthropocentric—it is based on the operation of the human being."[88]

Thucydides's human-centric approach to policy is evident in how he presents decision-making across the Hellenic world. In his account, "leaders and people, are anguishing over and are struggling to be good decision-makers, to reach the right decision, or the excellent, or the best decision."[89] This struggle was reflected in the nature of Hellenic politics itself. Hellenic *poleis* represented societies where politics was often, by nature, contentious. This was true across a variety of domestic systems ranging from the radical democracy of Periclean Athens through the oligarchies of Corinth and Sparta. In all these societies, debate was frequent and public and covered a variety of substantive and momentous issues. Thucydides offers a window into how choice and agency shaped decisions, particularly on the momentous topics of war and peace, which are at the heart of *The History*.

Choice through debate is front and center on two critical levels in Thucydides's work. First, he presents the perspectives of foreign representatives to a particular audience. Second, he also presents debates within individual societies. Sometimes these debates occur simultaneously. In Athens, Thucydides traces the debate within the Assembly about the decision to send aid to Corcyra even though the Athenians know that aiding Corcyra will bring tension (and possible conflict with Corinth). Representatives from both Corcyra and Corinth present their case in Athens before the Athenians debate and reach their decision to send aid to Corcyra.[90] It is clear in the context of this debate that there is no foregone conclusion. Athens could just as easily reject Corcyra's offer of alliance as accept it. Even in accepting to aid Corcyra, the Athenians were measured. They constructed a novel diplomatic solution—a purely defensive alliance—and sent a force of ten ships to aid in the defense of the city with limited rules of engagement.

Thucydides's account is full of such debates over foreign-policy choices. After the ensuing battle between the Corinthians and the Corcyraeans (aided by the Athenians), there is a debate in Sparta to determine whether the Athenians have broken their treaty obligations. Athenians, Corinthians, and Spartans speak on the two sides of the debate. The outcome is clearly not a foregone conclusion. Even members of the Spartan elite speak on both sides of the issue. Thucydides presents the Spartan king Archidamus speaking in favor of moderation, in opposition to the ephor Sthenelaidas, who argues in favor of war.[91] Later, the Athenians debate, in a highly contentious and often overlooked passage, what to do with the citizens of Mytilene after their revolt had been crushed. The demagogue Cleon advocates annihilation in the name of the empire. In opposition, the judicious Diodotus (successfully) recommends mercy and moderation in the name of the national interest.[92] The Assembly's decision is to overturn the order to annihilate Mytilene, although more than a thousand oligarchs are still executed. There are other numerous debates in Thucydides. Three of these debates are significant enough to warrant additional attention. These are the debate in Athens about whether to violate the spirit of the Peace of Nicias (concluded in 421) and pursue an alliance with Sparta's enemy Argos,[93] the debate over whether to send an expedition of conquest to Sicily,[94] and the debate in Sicily between the Syracusans and the Athenians in their attempt to win over the people of Camarina.[95] In each of these cases, no decision is a foregone conclusion, and "system-level" considerations are not front and center.

In Thucydides's account of the Sicilian expedition, Athens' elder statesman Nicias argues against the campaign on the grounds that Athens already has enough problems maintaining its security against existing threats. Alcibiades, the up-and-comer of Athenian politics, presents the opposite case. He advocates the expedition for glory, for empire, and on the basis that there is "no reasonable argument to induce us to hold back ourselves or to justify any excuse to our allies in Sicily for not helping them."[96] This debate is one of the longest Thucydides presents. It is immediately mirrored by a debate in Syracuse concerning whether to believe reports that a large Athenian force has been dispatched to Sicily and their presumed intent to attack Syracuse with an eye toward conquering the entire island. The debate at Camarina touches on many of Thucydides's core themes. In inviting the Camarinaeans into their alliance, the Syracusans present the specter of an Athenian conquest of all Sicily. Echoing the Corcyraeans of Book 1, they argue that Athens will conquer Syracuse first and then Camarina. This, we may recall, was the argument of the Corcyraeans to the Athenians: "Corinth has attacked us first in order to attack you afterwards."[97] The Athenians, on the other hand, press the argument that their interests align with those of Camarina for a partnership against the Syracusans. At the conclusion of the debate, both the Athenians and Syracusans leave empty handed. Hedging between their fear of Athenian imperialism and their hatred of the Syracusans, the Camarinaeans answer that they cannot help either side.[98]

The constant theme in these debates, and in others, is that the decision-makers had a conscious choice among several policy options. Very often, decisions were based not on overwhelming majorities but on narrow margins. Decisions, like the proposed annihilation of the citizens of Mytilene, could even be reversed. Such a course of events demonstrates a clear lack of inevitability. Examples, like the case of Mytilene, also show the centrality of domestic politics and domestic political systems in deciding policy. They force us to challenge a purely structural reading of Thucydides.

NOTES

1. Thuc. 1.23 (W).
2. Morley, "The Melian Dilemma," 2.
3. For a debate on the "necessity" vs. the "inevitability" of war see Kousk-ouvelis (2019). Warner (1972), for example, translates the passage with "inevitable." Hammond (2009) renders it as the reason "which forced the war."
4. Howard, *Causes of War*, 9–10.
5. Rahe, "The Primacy of Greece," 60.
6. Waltz, *Man, the State, and War*, 159.
7. Allison, *Destined for War*, 29.
8. Gilpin, *War and Change*; Gilpin, "The Theory of Hegemonic War."
9. Thuc. 1.23 (W).
10. Consider Thuc. 1.1 & 1.10 vs. 1.88 & 4.60.
11. Thuc. 1.118.
12. Gilpin, "The Theory of Hegemonic War," 595.
13. Kagan, *On the Origins of War and the Preservation of Peace*, 70.
14. Ibid.
15. Mark Kauppi, in *Hegemonic Rivalry from Thucydides to the Nuclear Age*, ed. Richard Ned Lebow and Barry Strauss (Boulder: Westview Press, 1991), 110 posits that we can challenge the designation of bipolarity but leaves matters there. Michael Doyle in *Ways of War and Peace*, (New York: W.W. Norton and Company, 1997), 71 tries to split the difference and describes the system as "quasi-bipolar."
16. Aron, *Peace and War*, 136–149.
17. Fleiss, *Thucydides and the Politics of Bipolarity*.
18. Forde, "Thucydides on Peace."
19. Santoro, "Bipolarity and War," 81.
20. Gilpin, "The Theory of Hegemonic War," 595; Gilpin, "Peloponnesian War and Cold War," 32.
21. Mearsheimer, *The Tragedy of Great Power Politics*, 358–359.
22. Platias and Koliopoulos, "Grand Strategies Clashing."
23. Gilpin, "Peloponnesian and Cold War," 32.
24. Ibid., 595.
25. Aron, *Peace and War*, 139.
26. Wagner, "What was bipolarity?" 78.

27. Waltz, "The Stability of a Bipolar World," 888.
28. Ibid.
29. Ibid., 892.
30. Doyle, *Ways of War and Peace*, 71.
31. Ibid., 72.
32. Cartledge, *The Spartans*, 86.
33. Thucydides (1.13.2) writes of a field army of 13,000 Athenian hoplites and an additional 16,000 hoplites, possibly *metics* or mercenaries, engaged in the defense of the cities or deployed as detachments.
34. Doyle, *Ways of War and Peace*, 71.
35. Cartledge, *Sparta and Lakonia*, 264.
36. The εἵλωτες (helots) were a population of Peloponnesian Greeks (from Messenia and Laconia) subjugated by the Spartans more than two centuries before Thucydides.
37. Wagner, "What was bipolarity?" 89.
38. Ibid.
39. Aron, *Peace and War*, 148.
40. Thuc. 6.1.
41. Wagner, "What was bipolarity?" 81.
42. Waltz, *Theory of International Politics*, 169.
43. Eckstein, *Mediterranean Anarchy, Interstate War, and the Rise of Rome*, 48.
44. Hanson, *A War Like No Other*, 13.
45. Athenians owned slaves outright. Spartans exploited the labor of helots, a subject population equivalent to medieval serfs, who were to all intents and purposes owned by the Spartan state. The question of whether helots were slaves in the modern sense is notorious for classicists and need not preoccupy us here. There is a more detailed analysis of Sparta's domestic system in chapter 3.
46. Waltz, *Theory of International Politics*, 169.
47. Thuc. 1.36–7.
48. Thuc. 1.82 (W).
49. Ibid., 1.71.
50. Thuc. 5.17.
51. Ibid., 5.31.
52. The work based on hegemonic transition theory (Gilpin) and "Thucydides's Trap" (Allison) are examples of the predominant view that Sparta was the status quo power and Athens the revisionist challenger. This characterization is reversed in the excellent article by Pla-

tias and Koliopoulos (2002) in which Athens is the status quo power and Sparta the revisionist power.

53. Kagan, *The Peloponnesian War*, 4.
54. Ibid., 5.
55. *War and Change in World Politics*, 29.
56. Rahe, *The Spartan Regime*, 9.
57. Thuc. 1.95.
58. Thuc. 1.95 (W).
59. *Homoioi* (Ὅμοιοι) is often the designation of these full Spartan citizens. Thucydides often, though not exclusively, uses the word Spartiates (Σπᾰρτῐᾱται), which the translation by Rex Warner renders as a member of "the Spartan officer class." This creates an unnecessary confusion because Thucydides also uses the word *arkhontes* (ἄρχοντες), a word more precisely translated in this context as officers, to denote command of one individual over others on the battlefield. *Arkhontes*, in other contexts can also mean lords or rulers. While Spartiates could and did command on the field, they were just as likely to serve in the ranks of the phalanx itself. Their position as "peers" was primarily a social and economic distinction, one that placed them at the very top of Spartan society. "Similars" is perhaps a more literal translation for *homoioi*, but, due to its artificial sound, it lacks the elegance of "peers," in our view.
60. Aristotle, *Politics* (Pol), 1270a15–1270b6.
61. Cartledge, *Sparta and Lakonia*, 264.
62. Herodotus, *The Histories*, 9.23.2–29.
63. Thuc. 2.107.
64. Ibid., 5.68.
65. Cartledge, *Sparta and Lakonia*, 264.
66. Thuc. 2.13.
67. Ibid., 1.25.
68. Ibid., 1.46.
69. Kagan, *The Peloponnesian War*, 59.
70. Thuc. 1.100.
71. Ibid., 2.7.
72. Kagan, *The Peloponnesian War*, 84.
73. de Ste. Croix, *The Origins of the Peloponnesian War*, 205–9.
74. Thuc. 4.3–6.
75. Ibid., 4.6.
76. Buck, *A History of Boeotia*, 144.
77. Thuc. 1.87.

78. de Ste. Croix, *The Origins of the Peloponnesian War*, 102–111.
79. There is also an interesting argument that the Spartans sought una-
    nimity to soothe their legalistic (and religious) worries that *they* were
    violating the treaty by attacking Athens. To meet legal and religious
    requirements, Athens had to be the aggressor and the state that violated
    the Thirty Years Peace. Unanimity among the allies would do much to
    smooth over these legal and religious fears.
80. Thuc. 1.122.
81. Thuc. 1.125 (W).
82. Ibid.
83. Thuc. 2.1.
84. Synder, "The Security Dilemma in Alliance Politics," 467.
85. Ibid.
86. Santoro, "Bipolarity and War," 76.
87. Jaffe, *Thucydides on the Outbreak of War*, 8.
88. Kouskouvelis, *Thucydides on Choice and Decision Making*, xvi.
89. Ibid., 169.
90. Thuc. 1.32–45.
91. Ibid., 1.66–88.
92. Ibid., 3.36–50.
93. Ibid., 5.43–46.
94. Ibid., 6.8–32.
95. Ibid., 6.76–88.
96. Thuc. 6.18 (W).
97. Ibid., 1.33.
98. Thuc. 6.88.

CHAPTER 3

POWER AND FEAR

LOOKING FOR DEEPER MEANINGS

"[I]n the test of action, when the element of fear is present, we fall short of our ideal."[1]

—Thucydides

"So we tried having the officers look at the factors that influenced the decisions of the Athenians and of the Spartans. This made them realize that the issues of whether to send a campaign overseas or not, whether to follow a maritime strategy or a land strategy, are that people have grappled with for many years. They are issues that are not easily resolved, but many of the fundamental considerations have not changed all that much, over these years."[2]

—Admiral Stansfield Turner

In the previous chapter, we addressed misinterpretations intrinsic to the systemic understanding of the material presented to us by Thucydides in *The History*. Our hope was to debunk, or at least weaken, the facile characterization of the Hellenic world as one defined by bipolarity and Spartan hegemony in which the origin of the war and critical decisions by various actors are explained as a function of those systemic factors. In this chapter, we will explore in greater depth two concepts underpinning Thucydides's analysis of the origins of war and international politics more generally: "power" and "fear." While power and fear in *The History* are most strongly associated with their presentation by Thucydides as *alethestate prophasis* (the truest underlying causes) of the war, this is neither the first nor the last time he engages with these fundamental issues and their relation to international politics. For Thucydides, power and fear are intimately linked. As Hermocrates of Syracuse points out: "superior powers [like Athens] are both envied and feared."[3] In *The History*, fear is not a simple motivation for one side vis-à-vis another. Instead, it is a perpetual feature of the international system exerting a continuous influence on various actors. To offer it as a general explanation for a particular conflict is therefore problematic. As a constant within the system it always exerts an influence. As with earlier concepts, it is a necessary but not sufficient condition for decisions. To explain a particular conflict, there must be a particular tangible fear that drives policymakers to action in a specific moment.

Power and fear are essential themes throughout Thucydides's work, reinforcing their timeless role in international politics. Thucydides ascribed their importance to the outbreak of the great war between Athens and Sparta and subsequent scholars have used them to explain behavior throughout history. When taken superficially, Thucydides's synthesis attributing the war to Spartan fear of Athenian power presents substantial support for his place as a source of the realist tradition. Realism continues to emphasize the role of "power" in international politics as opposed to norms. The pursuit of power—because of the fundamental characteristics of human beings (classical realism) and through the structural imperatives forced on us by our need for security and survival in an anarchical international system (structural realism or neo-realism)—means an enduring role for fear as an essential motivation for state behavior.

Thucydides, however, offers us far more than these simplifications imply. Using the evidence from his work in conjunction with the broader base of evidence about the ancient Hellenic world, we can more precisely identify the nature of Spartan fear. Athenian power and Spartan fear are central to Thucydides's famous line regarding the cause of the war, but he also tells readers much about Athenian fear and Spartan power beyond it. Unpacking these various subjects provides us with a more complete understanding of the actions of various players and, in turn, greater predictive power in looking at the motivators for state behavior. Spartan fears were centered on the brittle nature of their domestic political order and the disillusion of the alliances they depended on for their power. Both of these vulnerabilities were understood by Spartan policymakers. Athenian actions prompted Spartans to consider a response when these things were threatened.

Spartan power rested on their army, constrained as it was by the domestic limitations and foreign partnerships analyzed in chapter 2. The power of Sparta's army created its own vulnerabilities. The Spartan state was so dependent on its army that a major battlefield defeat could put the entire domestic order at risk. Athenian power, although significant, had its own limitations based on logistics and domestic factors. Like Sparta's army, Athens's fleet was the lifeblood of its city. Without a fleet to ensure its import of grain, the Athenian multitude would starve. The course of the war demonstrated that Athens could not survive without its fleet, but also that ships were easier to replace than men. Athenians, like Spartans, also had fears regarding the loyalty of their allies and clients. These fears also had a role to play in the war's origin and course.

This chapter will explore the nature of power (both Spartan and Athenian) as we understand the concept in Thucydides. It will also look at the meaning of Spartan fear. We seek to develop a more comprehensive understanding of power and fear as they are presented within *The History* and through our broader knowledge of the Hellenic world. We will also attempt to go beyond Thucydides's proposition of Spartan fear as a key underlying cause of the war to explore how fear applied to policymakers in general, including in Athens. Although ubiquitous in Thucydides's account, fear is not a prosaic concept. It motivates effective decision-making only if the fears themselves are rational and linked to real security threats. Decisions linked to irrational fears, or even to the hubristic disregard for fear, are dangerous.

At the same time, the richness of Thucydides's account shows us that power, even in the context of the Hellenic world, was difficult to measure and went beyond simple metrics of "hard power" such as the size of armies, the number of ships, or available financial resources. Throughout Thucydides's account, we find a more holistic approach to power, one that is directly applicable to our world today. We see how each source of power could at once be a strength and a weakness, that calculating power within international relations is always challenging, not only because of the inherently unpredictable nature of war (and events in general) but also because of the non-fungibility of most sources of power. Power is only relevant in terms of how it can be deployed in order to compel one side to do what the other wants. It is only useful as a concept for advocating policy to the extent to which we understand how it can further the desired outcomes of various actors.

Finally, in looking for the origins of the war, Thucydides offers us not merely the simplistic narrative of an established hegemon challenged by an upstart, but of competing great powers, which calculated that war offered the best way to preserve their preeminence and the allegiance of their allies and clients. While Athens was concerned with the loss of the seaborne trade on which its prosperity (and power) depended, Sparta feared the undermining of its domestic order and the defections of allies from its Peloponnesian league. These were the foundations of Sparta's power. Challenges to them were fundamental to Spartan security. Spartan perceptions of threat along these lines made Spartan policymakers willing to use war to protect its security.

POWER

In the previous chapter, we noted that the complexities of the ancient Hellenic world defied a simple bipolar characterization. The meaning of power, however, both as presented by Thucydides and in a more wide-ranging sense, will be dealt with here. What was power in the ancient world, and how did Thucydides think about it? It is straightforward to think of power in simplistic terms, basing assumptions on those things that can be measured most directly: population, the number of soldiers, the number of ships, territory, allies, and annual income. These metrics endure in modern analyses of international relations.[4] But these are simple metrics. As analytical tools they are blunt instruments. Nevertheless, we continue to use them even as we acknowledge their limitations. Thucydides was naturally familiar with these conceptions of power and does not shy away from using them to define and compare the strength of Athens and Sparta. But are they really the best means to capture the dynamics of power in international relations? Thucydides offers us a view into how these metrics do not, by themselves, explain the balance of power. He also acknowledged that even leaders within a state can misunderstand and miscalculate the power of their own state. As the Spartans, desperate to come to a negotiated settlement that would rescue their men trapped on the island of Sphacteria, humbly point out: "Our resources are the same as ever; we simply miscalculated them, and this is a mistake that may be made by everyone."[5]

Resources and power are easy to miscalculate for a number of reasons. First, there is a question of applicability. This principle is clearly demonstrated by the greatest strengths of the two combatants: Spartan land forces and the Athenian fleet. While these two factors were supreme in their respective domains, they both faced significant limitations in application against their respective foes. The Spartan army could not engage the Athenian fleet, much less defeat it. These same limitations applied to the Athenian fleet with regard to Sparta's army.

Second, power and resources also had structural limitations on their ability to inflict serious damage on the opposite power. Athens's fleet could sail around the Peloponnese, harming the trade of Sparta and its allies and landing Athenian forces to disrupt alliances, but it could not, on its own, break Spartan power. Sparta's army could (and did) invade Athenian territory. But the army could make no headway against the Long Walls protecting Athens and connecting it to the port of Piraeus. The primary strength of each power was thus rendered less useful than it had appeared at the very beginning of the conflict.

There were other limitations on Spartan power. As we discussed in the previous chapter, the Spartans confronted geographical constraints. The Isthmus of Corinth and the mountainous terrain between it and Attica meant that Spartan forces could not easily march on Athens without the support of Corinth and Megara. To wage war without either of these partners left the Spartans with the prospect of being bottled up in the Peloponnese or risking offensive amphibious operations in the face of Athenian naval superiority. Once they reached Attica, there were other concerns for a Spartan army. Although Spartan troops were supreme in the field, Thucydides, and other sources, make it clear that the Spartans lacked skills in siege warfare.[6] This made reducing the several border fortresses protecting Attica difficult and time consuming. A successful siege of Athens's Long Walls was even less feasible. The Spartans could lay siege to Athens, but they could not hope to breach its walls. Using a siege to play on starvation and public opinion were the only potentially effective weapons. Such an approach, however, would take time to have an impact. While the Long Walls stood and Athens maintained its fleet, Athens would be able to continuously import food and other necessary materials.

The potential effectiveness of a Spartan siege was undermined by the factor of time on another level too. Domestic tensions put another key constraint on Spartan military power. In the previous chapter, we addressed how Sparta was largely dependent on its allies to wage large-scale operations on land and especially at sea. Sparta's domestic political order—the order that provided the foundation for the unique social and economic structure—depended on the continued subjugation of the helots. Helots were essentially state-owned serfs. Most helots remained on their farms and in their villages, but their industry and agriculture were largely appropriated to supply Sparta's needs. Helot men also served Spartan citizens on the battlefield, managing equipment and supplies and sometimes even participating in combat. Helot women performed domestic work inside Spartan homes.

Their position as a permanent underclass meant that they were continually looking to overthrow their Spartan masters. After the devastating earthquake of 464, the Spartans' fear of a helot revolt led them to reach out to Athens for help. The Spartans then compounded their embarrassment by clumsily refusing the Athenians who arrived to render that aid in besieging the rebellious helots of Mt. Ithome.[7] Instead of welcoming the Athenians as experts in siege warfare, the Spartans instead became fearful that the Athenians would support the helots in their revolution, on the grounds of their democratic and "revolutionary" inclinations.[8] The Athenians were summarily dismissed. This contretemps was so damaging to Spartan-Athenian relations that the pro-Sparta Cimon (whose son Lacedaemonius[9] led the relief force) was ousted from power in Athens before the Athenian Assembly repudiated the terms of its alliance with Sparta in retaliation.[10]

Expelling the Athenians was grounded in Spartan paranoia over the possibility of a helot revolt. This fear kept its citizen army in a permanent state of military alert—*taga*. Each year, there was a ritual declaration of war against the helots so that Spartans could kill them without fear of any religious pollution.[11] Thucydides argues that the Spartans created most of their institutions with security vis-à-vis the helots in mind.[12] As a further control mechanism, Spartans severely restricted the entry of foreigners to their city, attempting to prevent the influx of possibly subversive ideas. A graphic demonstration of how this fear could manifest itself was given several years into the Peloponnesian War. When a series of reverses made the Spartans feel particularly vulnerable to domestic revolution, Thucydides claims that they took two thousand helots who showed the most spirit—and were therefore thought to be the most likely to revolt—and simply murdered them.[13]

This was not the only occasion when Sparta policy was dictated by the fear of a helot revolt. During the Peloponnesian War, Athens landed a substantial force at Pylos and fortified the area, looking to encourage the Messinian helots to revolt. The Spartan army in Attica immediately abandoned its annual invasion of Athenian territory and returned home to the Peloponnese after a campaign of only two weeks.[14] For Sparta's militaristic and stratified society, the home front was always the most vulnerable. Athens—democratic, enterprising, largely secure against land-based invasion, and maneuverable at sea—was perfectly positioned to exploit Sparta's weaknesses.

Even the army, Sparta's greatest strength, was a brittle tool for projecting power. The manpower shortage that characterized Spartan society made deploying the army on campaign a risky proposition. Unlike Athens, Sparta had no walls to protect it. Unlike Athens, it had no great stores of wealth from silver or gold mines, revenues from trade, or tribute. Sparta's army was the single most important component of its power. Spartan commanders therefore, confronted the strategic reality Winston Churchill once applied to Admiral John Jellicoe during the First World War. As the commander of Britain's fleet, he was, according to Churchill, "the only man on either side who could lose the war in an afternoon."[15] Spartan commanders were in a similar position of responsibility and vulnerability. They wielded Sparta's greatest weapon but also confronted the risk of losing the war, indeed of losing everything, "in an afternoon."

The larger the force of Spartans deployed, the greater this risk became. To mitigate this risk, Spartan *homoioi* (peers) were typically deployed in small numbers as a leavening agent in larger forces. These armies would have contingents of allies and characteristically a representation from the various classes of the Spartan system: Spartiate *homoioi*, *hypomeiones* (Spartans lacking full political rights), *perioikoi* (affiliated neighbors), and helots. That the life of each of Sparta's *homoioi* was highly valued by the state is clear from their reaction to the Athenian capture of one hundred and twenty men of this class at Sphacteria. As Thucydides records, securing the return of these men was a primary driver for Sparta's offer of an armistice to Athens in 423.[16] In this case, we see that the potential loss of even a small contingent of *homoioi* was enough to prompt calls for peace.

A single defeat involving a major Sparta force had the potential to bring the entire system crumbling down. Spartan commanders thus risked a great deal when they confronted foes on the battlefield—far more than their Athenian counterparts risked. As a result of these limitations, we see that major battles involving large numbers of Spartan forces were rare. Such set-piece battles, while showcasing Sparta's greatest comparative advantage, were also the most perilous for the long-term health of the state. When they occurred, however, the Spartans tended to live up to their fearsome reputation. Throughout the fifth century, victories over the Persians (at Plataea in 479), the Athenians (at Tanagra in 457), and the Athenians and Argives (at Mantinea 418), confirmed the fearsome reputation of the *homoioi* on the battlefield.

The ruling class of peers were keenly aware of these critical vulnerabilities. So were Sparta's enemies. Alcibiades—the Athenian aristocrat and imperialist who played a prominent role in Athenian politics from the Peace of Nicias to the Sicilian expedition (421–415)—argued, in defense of his political acumen, that he had "made the Spartans risk their all on the issue of one day's fighting at Mantinea."[17] According to Thucydides, at this battle in 418 there were three thousand five hundred Spartans within an army of nine thousand against eight thousand Argives, Athenians, and their allies. We do not know what proportion of the three thousand five hundred Spartans were *homoioi*. Thucydides's account suggests that while not all three thousand five hundred present were peers, they made up a majority at this particular battle.[18] Half a century later at Leuktra (371) and at the second Battle of Mantinea (362), the losses suffered by Sparta's army irrevocably shattered the power of the state. As with the vulnerabilities of the home front and Sparta's dependence on its allies, so with the nature of its army itself. From these factors, we see that calculating the power of Sparta was not as easy an exercise either for the ancient Greeks or for modern scholars. The same is true of Athens.

Like Spartan power, Athenian power was not obviously supreme, nor was its source of strength without accompanying weaknesses. Athens was rightfully considered the most powerful single Greek state, in no small part because of its wealth and population size.[19] Athenian soldiers had a fearsome reputation in battle, no doubt partially earned through their performance at the Battle of Marathon in 490. By the time of the Peloponnesian War, the Athenian fleet was a superior fighting force, having demonstrated its dominance in successive victories against both Greek and Persian opposition.

Naval warfare was far more expensive than land warfare and so wealth was the essential component underpinning Athens's fleet. It also allowed Athens to replace ships quickly and recover from setbacks. As Thucydides explains through Pericles, a large part of the funding came from the money paid in tribute by its allies.[20] But Athens also grew rich through taxing the enormous amount of trade that passed through its port at Piraeus and from court duties assessed from its highly litigious society. Athens's egalitarian mode of democracy was further reinforced through the requirement that leading Athenian citizens contribute frequently to the public purse, either through regular taxes, special wartime levies, or through the required "donations" of public services and entertainments.[21] In order to propagate a degree of equality, the richest Athenian citizens had significant financial obligations to their society. Elites both embraced these costs as evidence of their devotion to the public and chafed against them.

Athenian power was thus a function of economic power, military power, and international influence. Its growth, which supposedly constituted the truest cause of the war, requires a much deeper analysis, particularly because it is treated with some ambiguity both by Thucydides and within the secondary literature. Thucydides paints a picture of Athens as a growing power, challenging Sparta for dominance with the Hellenic world, but this is only part of the picture. His evidence is somewhat contradictory. While arguing that Athens was growing and that this caused concern among the Spartans, he also describes Athens as an already dominant force. Corinthian envoys characterize Athens as stronger than any other single *polis.* Thucydides describes "the greater part of Hellas" as already "under the control of Athens."[22] Part of these claims are exaggerations made to support a line of argument by Athens's enemies, but Thucydides's direct claim of Athenian supremacy is overstated to say the least. It also paints a confusing picture over the "rise of Athenian power." Part of the explanation lies in the analysis we have already presented about the limitations of Sparta. Sparta, if we restrict the term to the *polis* itself and its proper citizens, was not as powerful as Athens. To match the men of Attica, Sparta needed its *perioikoi* partners and its helots. To match the Delian League, it needed all the allies it could find in the Peloponnese and beyond. Neither Athens nor Sparta was a hegemon in the sense of the term as applied in modern IR theory. They were hegemons in the literal sense of the Greek word hegemon —leader. They were the leaders of alliance blocs. Neither was superior to the other in an empirical sense that could accurately capture their potential and power.

Thucydides presents his readers with a description of the rise of Athens focusing on the period between the battle of Salamis (480) and the outbreak of the Peloponnesian War (431). This "50-year period"—or *Pentecontaetia* as Thucydides calls it—is defined by the rise of Athenian power. But while Athens did establish an empire in the form of the Delian League, the trajectory of its power was not entirely upwards. Between 480 and 431, Athens had its share of both success and failure.

While Athens was able to establish the Delian League and grow it into an Athenian Empire, it also suffered battlefield reversals and diplomatic defeats. This is an important historical fact to recognize. It undermines the argument Thucydides presents, through the Corinthians, depicting Athens as the dominant Hellenic power. It contradicts the simplistic narrative of an uninterrupted Athenian rise. As usual, when we dig a little more deeply into Thucydides, we see that Athenian power did not rise in a linear fashion. It moved forward in fits and starts. It was checked and undermined and it even declined in territorial terms. Thucydides would certainly have known and understood this. Athenian "power" vis-à-vis Sparta remains unreconciled throughout his account.

Finally, the historical record presents evidence to contradict the view that Sparta did nothing in the face of Athens's rise until the fateful decision for war in 432. In this case, we see one of the earlier challenges in reading Thucydides identified earlier in our introduction. The argument that Sparta did nothing is not Thucydides's argument, but the argument that he puts in the mouths of the Corinthian emissaries to Sparta. Nevertheless, the premise of Spartan inaction is accepted uncritically by modern scholars, even though Thucydides presents substantial evidence to contradict this point. Accepting the Corinthian accusation of Spartan inaction at face value is hardly defensible in light of the fact that Sparta fought a war against Athens only a quarter of a century before the great Peloponnesian War. Thucydides both lived through and wrote about this earlier conflict. The "great' Peloponnesian War that was the subject of his *The History* was therefore not an isolated conflict but the second of a brace.

Modern scholars have largely ignored the First Peloponnesian War and the efforts (sometimes successful) of Sparta and its allies to contain Athenian power during the *Pentecontaetia*. One reason for the lack of attention given to these previous actions against the rise of Athenian power is the paucity of time Thucydides spends on the subject. Perhaps it is a subject to which he would have returned and fleshed out had he completed his history. Some historians suggest he overlooked it largely because it was a war fought primarily between Athens and Sparta's allies (Corinth and Thebes) and involved only a few direct clashes between Athenian and Spartan forces.[23] From the patchy evidence that we have, all indications are that the fighting was sporadic. The overall form of the campaigns is even more difficult to determine because we lack documentary sources for the period. Thucydides was in a position to tell us more but failed to do so. His omission has drawn criticism[24] and fairly so. The First Peloponnesian War was not an insignificant conflict. Many of the key relationships and causes of the later war were already present in this first conflict. Understanding the context of this first war adds key elements to our story. We see the pattern of Spartan allies (in this case Thebes at the head of the Boeotian Confederacy but also Corinth) leading a war against Athens. We see Sparta responding to the initiatives of its allies and eventually committing its soldiers against Athens. And we see Athens pressured by revolt and instability within its empire.

During the quarter century before the Corcyra crisis, that is to say, during the First Peloponnesian War and its aftermath, the Athenians experienced mixed fortunes. As a result, in the run-up to the outbreak of the great Peloponnesian War, Athenian territorial power had not grown.[25] Through their initial successes, they had won a land empire in Boeotia. After a series of subsequent defeats at the hands of Sparta and the Boeotian League, they were forced to relinquish these newly won territories. During the same time that their power in Boeotia declined, the Athenians had to fight to subdue rebellious client states within the Delian League. An ambitious expedition to Egypt to aid in a revolt against the Persian empire was also defeated in 454 with significant losses.[26] These setbacks challenge the narrative of an unhampered rise of Athenian power facilitated by Spartan dithering.

In spite of the prevailing narrative, Sparta and its allies acted against Athens early on. Opposition to Athens existed both within Sparta and, critically, among Sparta's most powerful allies. It is simply incorrect to argue, in the manner of some modern scholars, that "[p]rior to their imbroglio with Corcyra [433-432], Corinth evinced no hostility to Athens or fear of its power."[27] This view is directly contradicted by the fact that Corinth and Athens fought a war against each other in 460–457.[28] These hostilities were brutal and hardly forgettable. In one engagement near Megara, the Athenians trapped a large contingent of retreating Corinthians in an enclosure surrounded by a ditch on a private estate and "stoned to death all who were inside."[29]

Nor were the Spartans as indolent as Thucydides's Corinthian envoys accused them of being. We should not accept claims of Spartan inaction from modern scholars, which flow from this flawed picture. It was not the case that "Sparta failed to arrest the growth of Athenian power."[30] Nor is the simplified narrative defensible that "Sparta could have prevented the growth of Athenian power, but she failed to do so."[31] On the contrary, Sparta plotted with Thasos to begin dismembering the Delian League as early as 461–460.[32] Sparta's army took the field and defeated the Athenians at Tanagra in 457. Sparta's allies, led by Thebes, confronted the Athenians at Coronea in 447, defeated them, and won back Boeotia from the Delian League. Thucydides, and the broader historical record, demonstrate the challenges confronting rising new powers, both from regional balancers (in this case, Thebes and Corinth) and the other major powers in the system (in this case, Sparta).

The struggle of the Athenians with the Spartans and their allies between 460 and 431 hints at the strengths and weaknesses of Athenian power. During this time, Athens already had a formidable fleet. It had a large and capable army, but this force was still outmatched by Sparta's hoplites. Athens could mobilize enormous resources, but renewing these resources was still dependent on tribute, trade, and support from its allies and clients within the Delian League. Some of these partners were more reliable than others, and a few already regarded Athens's empire as nothing more than a tyranny, as Thucydides famously argued through Pericles.[33] So, what were the foundations of Athenian power, which allowed it to establish and sustain this empire?

The foundation of Athenian power was its large population. By population size, it was the largest *polis* in the ancient world. In comparison, Thucydides tells us, Sparta was little more than a collection of villages. We have already addressed the manpower shortage that limited Sparta's power projection. Athens, on the other hand, had an abundant population of citizens. Like Sparta's, Athenian society was stratified. At the top were Athenian citizens. While Sparta's requirements of wealth meant that some citizens (*homoioi*) were more equal than others (*hypomeiones*), Athenian citizens enjoyed a theoretical equality regardless of wealth and access to various state offices. As alluded to earlier, there was significant economic inequality among citizens, but programs to enforce significant contributions to the public sphere by the richest citizens tried to remediate these inequalities.

Below the citizens were resident aliens, or metics.[34] Metics were foreign residents who worked at various skilled jobs and as entrepreneurs. In exceptional circumstances they might become wealthy. Although they could not own property in Attica, they did pay taxes to the state and enjoyed limited access to Athens's robust legal system. Those who could afford the necessary equipment served in the military as hoplites and the rest as light troops. Occasionally, Athenian citizenship was bestowed on them as a special gift. Slaves were at the bottom rung of the Athenian social order. These men, women, and children lacked almost all political rights, but they were an essential feature of the Athenian economy because of their skilled and manual labor. We get a glimpse of their importance when Thucydides explains that the Spartan fortification of the nearby town of Decelea later in the war "was one of the chief reasons for the decline of Athenian power... more than 20,000 slaves, the majority of whom were skilled workmen, deserted, and all the sheep and farm animals were lost."[35]

Athenian citizens and residents were thus a numerous body from which the state could draw for service on the battlefield or at sea. Wealth dictated the branch of service for Athenian men of military age.

Service was a requirement for all male citizens but so was providing the necessary equipment. As a result, the wealthiest served in high office and as commanders. The wealthy might choose to ride to battle as part of the cavalry. The middle class could afford the panoply of the hoplite: a heavy, round shield made of wood with a bronze rim or bronze outer coating, helmet, armor, and spear. These hoplites served in the phalanx or as marines on ships. The poor (those who did not own property and worked for wages) lacked these resources. They served as light troops or, more often, were "volunteered" for service in the navy along with the poorer metics and mercenaries (a common element in the Hellenic world). Their most common service in the navy was in the capacity of rowers.

The very size of Athens's population was both a strength and a weakness. Between 430 and 426, the dense concentration of people within Athens at least exacerbated, and perhaps caused, the terrible plague. Thucydides recounts how this awful outbreak not only dealt a significant blow to Athenian manpower and confidence but also tore at the very fabric of Athenian society.[36] Athens's enormous population was also a challenge to feed. Thucydides, among other writers, emphasizes the poverty of the soil of Attica.[37] The poor agricultural yield of Attic soil made Athens (and its enormous population) reliant on the import of almost all significant raw materials. These included timber and other materials for ship building as well as basic foodstuff to feed the population.

Athens's vast population of "citizens, metics and slaves was fed by imported corn [grain] to a far greater extent than that of any other important Greek city."[38] This dependence on foreign sources of food directly influenced Athenian foreign and military policy. It is no accident that repeated and significant Athenian military expeditions went to places like Egypt, the Black Sea, Cyprus, and Sicily—all major sources of grain. A dependency on important food dovetailed with Athens's need to maintain naval supremacy. As long as Athens had command of the sea, it could import the food necessary to feed its population. Without a fleet, it would be vulnerable to being starved into submission through a siege—as happened following the defeat at Aegospotami at the very end of the war. Just as Sparta feared losing its allies, knowing that without them it could not project its power or maintain its domestic order, Athens feared losing its maritime lifeline and being starved into the status of second-rate power. Thus, we anticipate the discussion of fear to which we can now turn.

FEAR

As with power, so too fear plays an important role in Thucydides's *The History*. One contemporary scholar of philosophy has gone so far as to describe *The History* as "from one angle a meditation upon fear —its varieties, ubiquity, potency, and even rational necessity."[39] Fear, after all, is "the most important incentive to the formation of treaties, alliances, states, and eventually empires" in Thucydides's account.[40] Thucydides highlights this when the envoys of Mytilene argue to the Spartans that "in an alliance the only safe guarantee is an equality of mutual fear."[41] Thucydides uses various forms of three primary words —*phobos, deos,* and *ekplixis*[42]—to describe fear.[43] *Phobos*, which we can translate as fear or terror, appears no fewer than forty-four times in *The History*. Thucydides, of course, relies on Spartan fear (the second use of *phobos* in his text) for his explanation of the Spartan declaration of war.[44] Thucydides's attribution of the cause of the war to the fear felt by Sparta at the growth of Athenian power has sparked some of the most seminal debates concerning *The History* among both historians and political scientists.[45] These debates often center on the accuracy of Thucydides's analysis and the utility of his differentiating *aitiai* (the proximate grievances) from *prophasis* (an underlying cause).

While these debates, and similar ones, rage, an analysis of the elements defining Spartan fear is less common. International relations theory can tell us that Sparta feared the loss of its security. From human nature and from the Spartan hegemony we interpret from Thucydides, we can explain its fears in terms of losing its position of dominance within the Peloponnese. Beyond this, there is little analysis. Such explanations lack the degree of detail and precision appropriate to such momentous decisions of war and peace among great powers. This section will attempt to answer the key question of *what* Sparta feared and to use this analysis to make sense of its decision for war. At the same time, the impact of fear on decisions of Athenian policy is even less scrutinized, in spite of the fact that Thucydides repeatedly presents fear as an important driver for policy decisions. Although the main character in the drama of fear is Sparta, there is plenty of evidence within Thucydides to develop a picture of how *Athenian* fears also played a major role in the outbreak of war. To paraphrase Thucydides, Athenian fear is perhaps the most significant, though least talked about, factor in understanding the Peloponnesian War. This section will also grapple with identifying and analyzing the elements of Athenian fear and exploring how these fears influenced the outbreak of war.

> Fear was an important part of Sparta's identity in spite of their warrior ethos. As Plutarch records: the Lacedaemonians have temples of Death, Laughter, and that sort of thing, as well as of Fear. And they pay honors to Fear, not as they do the other powers which they try to avert because they think them baleful, but because they believe that fear [sic] is the chief support of their polity.[46]

Given their reputation for courage and martial valor, Sparta's relationship with fear is curious. Plutarch provides a starting point, but there is plenty of evidence to corroborate his analysis. The Spartan relationship with fear becomes more comprehensible when analyzed in the context of Sparta's domestic and international political system. Our description of the roots of Spartan power earlier in this chapter illustrates strong foundations but also critical vulnerabilities. It provides an implicit argument for the importance of fear to the Spartan polity. The perennial weakness relating to the subjugation of the helot population was a primary concern for Sparta, as was the fundamentally unequal political system, which created resentment among all classes not considered peers.

Both Xenophon and Aristotle, each an astute and admiring observer of
Sparta, noted the fear Spartans had of their helot population. Xenophon
famously recorded the desire of the helots to eat the Spartans "raw."[47]
This quote is often presented in a way that focuses its application only
to the helots, who occupied the very bottom of Spartan society. But this
decontextualizes Xenophon's primary point. He applied this appetite
for Spartan sashimi practically universally and said it was shared by all
of the classes below the *homoioi*: *neodamodes* (freedmen), *hypomeiones*
(Spartans lacking full political rights), and *perioikoi* (affiliated neighbors).
This suggests, at least, that the entire Spartan order rested on a powder
keg of social unrest. Marxist historians, naturally enough, have been
quick to point out this class antagonism and label it a key source of
Spartan weakness.[48] Whether the *homoioi* constituted a hated one percent
or not, there were real social tensions between those who qualified as
full citizens of Spartan society and all the rest.

Marxism and present discussions on economic inequality aside, we
know that class antagonism was commonplace in ancient societies,
appearing as a repeated source of social tensions. We have a vast body
of historical evidence addressing issues of property ownership, political
rights, and other social tensions in both Athens and Rome. From these
examples and what we know about Spartan society, we can assume that
Sparta was not exempt from such problems. On the contrary, it seems
to have been a society in which this conflict was particularly sharp.
Reinforcing Xenophon, Aristotle observed that the helots, in particular,
were "constantly awaiting [the] misfortunes [of the Spartans] as if in
ambush."[49] Thucydides, too, comments on this, famously describing
Sparta's domestic institutions as defined by fear (particularly of the
helots) and argued that their policy "with regard to the helots had always
been based almost entirely on the idea of security."[50]

Fear in the broader sense was at the root of Sparta's deep conservatism.
Sparta had fears relating to both its domestic order and its foreign
relations. Domestically, Sparta feared that opposition to its dominance

would weaken its grip on client states and the helot population. If these dependents and serfs rose up to challenge Spartan rule, it would be difficult for Sparta to maintain its power. It was indeed the revolt of numerous *perioikoi* in conjunction with the Messinian helots that irreparably broke Spartan power in 370–362.[51] This was what Sparta feared and this was what Spartan policy and its domestic institutions were designed to prevent.

Internationally, Sparta had to maintain its position as the hegemon of the Peloponnesian League. Its fear was that another power—Corinth, Argos, or even Athens—could displace it as the leader among the *poleis* of the Peloponnese. Thucydides alludes to this in an extremely insightful but often ignored passage about the cause of the war. Far less quoted than his line about Spartan fear and Athenian power is a subsequent argument presented by Thucydides about the cause of the war. Later in Book 1, he argued that:

> the point was reached when Athenian strength attained a peak plain for all to see and the Athenians began to encroach upon Sparta's allies. It was at this point that Sparta felt the position to be no longer tolerable and decided by starting this present war to employ all her energies in attacking and, if possible, destroying the power of Athens.[52]

In this passage, Thucydides could not be more clear. It was not Athenian power, *per se*, that troubled Sparta; it was the encroachment of Athenian power "upon Sparta's allies" that was intolerable. This, in Thucydides's view, is what "compelled" the Spartans to fight.

An explanation framed in terms of the threat Athens posed to Sparta's allies is far more persuasive than a generalized fear of Athenian power. This argument is supported by the historical record. Sparta, after all, did not oppose Athens as it assumed leadership of the Hellenic confederacy and took the war to Persia between 478 and 465. This rise of Athenian power, characterized by adventures in Ionia and victories against the Persians, was not troubling to Sparta. After 465, however, when Athenian power turned towards the *poleis* of the Hellenic world, matters changed. As we addressed earlier, Sparta was tempted to confront Athens over the revolt of Thasos and supported its allies, Thebes and Corinth, against Athens during the First Peloponnesian War.

Preserving alliances was at the heart of Spartan policy at the outbreak of the great Peloponnesian War as well. It provides a coherent explanation for why Sparta went to war with Athens and why it did so in 431 as opposed to at another time in its history. That Sparta's primary concern was its allies is reinforced directly by the speech of the hawkish ephor Sthenelaidas during the debate in Sparta that resulted in the Spartans declaring that the Athenians had broken its treaty obligations. In a truly laconic manner, Sthenelaidas's entire speech takes no more than a paragraph. But in those few lines, he mentions allies five times. Moreover, allies are used to underpin every point of his argument. He begins by accusing Athens of acting aggressively towards Sparta's allies. He justifies Sparta's power to counter Athens in terms of its own "good allies" who should not be betrayed to the Athenians. Instead, he argues, they are obliged to "come to the help of [their] allies quickly." And he concludes his speech with the exhortation for the Spartans, again, to not "betray" their allies.[53]

It was the nature of the Spartan system, its domestic limitations combined with the dynamics of the Peloponnesian League, which created this dependence of Sparta on its allies in foreign affairs and its helots for domestic security. These factors necessitated a confrontational response to Athens during the crisis over Corcyra in 432–431. Key allies such as Corinth were drifting from their loyalty to Sparta and were afraid that Sparta would be unable to protect them against Athens. In retaliation, Corinth made clear its intentions to abandon their alliance with Sparta and adopt neutrality or even a partnership with Athens. Such an event would isolate Sparta and reduce its capabilities significantly. At the same time, because Sparta's domestic institutions were so fragile, it could not afford to lose its position of primacy within the Peloponnesian League without seeing the entire domestic edifice of its power under severe threat. War was thus necessary, in the Thucydidean sense, to maintain Sparta's power. Without agreeing to wage war against Athens, Spartan power would have likely crumbled from within, beginning with Corinth's defection from the Peloponnesian League. This was the heart of Spartan fear. Without addressing the key role of Corinth, one modern historian nevertheless accurately identifies that Sparta feared "those things that [threatened] her regime and the way of life that [nourished] it."[54]

In spite of the centrality of Spartan fear, the decision for war was, nonetheless, the result of a complex story in which Athenian fears played a critical role. Leaving aside the unique helot factor, Sparta's fears had substantial overlap with those of Athens. Like Sparta, Athens had fears about the durability of its imperial construction—the Delian League. It feared revolts from among its client states.[55] It feared coalitions that would be superior to its own power, particularly increases in the power of Sparta's allies at sea.[56] It feared a loss of political autonomy (to Spartan pressure or to Persian influence). These fears, after all, as Thucydides explains, contributed to the *aitiai* (immediate grievances) for the war.

While Spartan fear has pride of place in Thucydides's account of the origins of the war and subsequent historical inquiries, Athenian fear is just as relevant to understanding events. Athenian fear is present not only as an explanation for conflict between Athens and Sparta but also for the establishment of the Athenian Empire itself. As the Spartans debated war or peace with Athens in 432, the Athenians present in Sparta openly acknowledged, in language with a familiar construction, that it was a "fear of Persia," which "compelled" Athens to "increase" its power. This was the "chief motive" behind the creation of its empire.[57] In this argument, fear is a necessary spur to action. It is a normal and logical motivation for significant policy decisions. Later in Thucydides's work, fear plays a role in the arguments presented by the Athenians to the Melians and is offered as an explanation for Athenian imperialism to the Camarinaeans in Sicily.[58]

We see Athenian fear at play in other stages along the road to war. When the Corcyraeans presented themselves in Athens to ask for an alliance against Corinth, their "most powerful appeal...was to fear."[59] The Corcyraeans warned the Athenians that "[i]f Corinth gets control of us first and you allow our navy to be united with hers, you will have to fight against the combined fleets of Corcyra and the Peloponnese."[60] To maintain its dominance at sea, Athens took sides in the Corcyraean civil war, largely out of the fear of the growth of Corinthian power. But Athenian fear had another impact on their foreign policy. They did not simply agree to a full offensive and defensive alliance with Corcyra, as was customary in the Hellenic world. Instead, because Athens feared the potential for a Spartan reaction to their involvement in the affairs of Corcyra and Corinth, they adopted a novel and moderate policy. After two days of debate, rather than the usual one, the Athenians made a proposal for "an alliance [with Corcyra] that was defensive only (*epimachia*)." As far as we know, this was an innovation in Greek diplomacy.[61] The terms of the *epimachia* meant that Athenian forces would only engage if Corcyra were attacked and would remain neutral in any conflict in which Corcyra were the aggressor. An Athenian force of ten ships was sent to Corcyra. In an attempt to placate Sparta, it was commanded by Lacedaemonius, the son of the pro-Spartan politician, Cimon. The rules of engagement for the fleet were highly restrictive. They were "to avoid battle with the Corinthians except... if the Corinthians sailed against Corcyra with the intention of landing on the island itself or at any point in Corcyraean territory."[62] As Thucydides emphasizes, "[t]hese instructions were given in order to avoid breaking the existing treaty [with Sparta]."[63] This policy aimed to avoid (or at least contain) war. It was, as one modern scholar argues, "a precisely crafted diplomatic device meant to bring the Corinthians to their sense without war."[64] In other words, it was an attempt at deterrence. And it was made because Athens, for all its power, did not want war with Sparta and feared the costs that such a conflict might entail.

Like many clever political stratagems, it also placed Athens in something of a win-win situation. If the Spartans refrained from action in spite of Athenian aid to Corcyra against Corinth, the Spartans would be humiliated in front of their allies. This could prompt defections within the Peloponnesian League. If, on the other hand, the Spartans chose to respond to the Athenian provocation, they would have to claim that the treaty had been broken and so take the responsibility for initiating a major war. Shouldering such a burden was no easy thing.

Time and again, in Thucydides, we see that fear is a fundamental motivation. According to one contemporary scholar, in *The History*, "248 decisions are directly or unambiguously explained by fear."[65] The relationship between decision-makers and fear remains a fraught one in Thucydides. Pericles warns the Athenian *demos* to refuse to retract the Megarian Decree at Sparta's demand, on the grounds that "[i]f you give in, you will immediately be confronted with some greater demand, since they will think that you only gave way on this point through fear."[66] This sentiment is echoed by Hermocrates of Syracuse, who declares that "[n]o one is forced into war by ignorance, nor, if he thinks he will gain from it, is he kept out of it by fear. The fact is that one side thinks that the profits to be won outweigh the risks to be incurred, and the other side is ready to face danger rather than accept an immediate loss."[67] Fear should be an important component in a policymaker's thought process. There should be a rational fear of the unknown future, of uncertainty and chance, as Hermocrates argues to the citizens of Syracuse, and this should be a brake on action because "if we all fear it alike, we shall think twice before we attack each other."[68]

For Thucydides, fear is not a sound basis for decision-making by itself. Leaders must distinguish between different kinds of fears and control their passions. There are rational fears that should inform policymakers, as when Athens created its empire. At the same time, irrational fears should not be allowed to overtake policymakers. Acting on baseless or exaggerated fears drives policymakers to mistakes. Finally, the absence of fear is also problematic. Without the guideposts of rational fear, decision-makers are vulnerable to hubris. They make mistakes. Thucydides illustrates this obliquely in the famous Melian Dialogue. Presented immediately before the Athenian decision to sail in force to Sicily with the goal of conquering Syracuse and "if possible" the entire island, the dialogue is a chilling lesson in how leaders oblivious to the warnings of fear can lead their states to destruction.[69] In successive interjections, the Athenians deny fearing: the end of their empire, Spartan power, opposition from Greeks living on islands, or even the justice of the gods.[70] Heady with hubris, they decided the fate of Melos and set their sights on Sicily, oblivious to the intractability of the inescapable Nemesis. To discuss Sicily, however, is to anticipate chapter 5 prematurely. Power and fear, with all the complexity they present in Thucydides, remain important factors in key decisions of state. Power and fear are often at the heart of alignment shifts, changing alliance dynamics, and great power politics more broadly. These subjects will be dealt with in greater detail in chapter 4.

NOTES

1. Thuc. 1.120.
2. Admiral Stansfield Turner, "Address to Chicago Council Navy League of the United States Lake Shore Club," March 9, 1973.
3. Thuc. 6.78 (W).
4. For example, see P. Kennedy, *The Rise and Fall of the Great Powers* and Wohlforth, "The Stability of the Unipolar World," 10.
5. Thuc. 4.18.
6. Ibid., 1.102.
7. Ibid., 1.101–102.
8. Thuc. 1.102 (W).
9. Literally someone from Lacedaemon or "Spartan." Naming his son "Spartan" was a concrete manifestation of Cimon's pro-Spartan orientation and policy.
10. de Ste. Croix, *The Origins of the Peloponnesian War*, 180–181.
11. Cartledge, *Sparta and Lakonia*, 15.
12. Thuc. 4.60.
13. Ibid., 4.80.
14. Ibid., 4.6.
15. Heathcote, *The British Admirals of the Fleet 1734–1995*, 130.
16. Thuc. 4.117 and 5.15.
17. Thuc. 6.16 (W).
18. Thuc. 5.66–67. There is a scholarly debate over the composition of Spartan armies involving both the numbers of *homoioi* relative to the other classes as well as whether or not they were deployed in mixed units. For example, see Cameron Hawkins, "Spartans and *Perioikoi*: The Organization and Ideology of the Lakedaimonian Army in the Fourth Century B.C.E.," *Greek, Roman, and Byzantine Studies*, 51 (2011), 401–434.
19. Thuc. 4.60.
20. Ibid., 2.13.
21. Kagan, *The Fall of the Athenian Empire*, 110–111.
22. Thuc. 1.88 (W).
23. de Ste. Croix, *The Origins of the Peloponnesian War*, 51.
24. Ibid., 50.
25. Kagan, *On the Origins of War and the Preservation of Peace*, 57.
26. Thuc. 1.104, 109.

27. Lebow, *The Tragic Vision of Politics*, 83.

28. Thuc. 1.104, 109.

29. Ibid., 1.106.

30. Gilpin, *War and Change in World Politics*, 90.

31. Jaffe, *Thucydides on the Outbreak of War*, 64.

32. Rahe, *The Spartan Regime*, 61.

33. Thuc. 2. 63.

34. μέτοικοι.

35. Thuc. 7.27 (W).

36. Thuc. 2.48–54.

37. Ibid., 1.2.5.

38. de Ste. Croix, *The Origins of the Peloponnesian War*, 46.

39. Desmond, "Lessons of Fear," 359.

40. Ibid., 363.

41. Thuc. 3.1 (W).

42. Φόβος (*phobos*) is translated as fear or terror and is almost synonymous with δέος (*deos*). *Deos* can have a context of foreboding to distinguish it from *phobos*. *Ekplixis* (ἐκπληξης) is fear in the sense of shock, trauma, or amazement and denotes a context of surprise.

43. Desmond, "Lessons of Fear," 361.

44. Thuc. 1.23, 1.88.

45. See, for example: de Ste. Croix 1972; Rhodes 1987; Gilpin 1991; Kauppi 1991; Kagan 1995; Ahrensdorf 1997; Bagby 1994, 2000; Lebow 2003; Bagnall 2004; Hanson 2005; Desmond 2006; Jaffe 2017; and Kouskouvelis 2019.

46. Plutarch, *Life of Cleomenes*, 9.1.

47. Xenophon, *Hellenica*, 3.3.

48. de Ste. Croix, *The Origins of the Peloponnesian War*, 90.

49. Aristotle, *Pol.* 2.9.39–40.

50. Thuc. 4. 80 (W).

51. Cartledge, *Sparta and Lakonia*, 228.

52. Thuc. 1.118 (W).

53. Ibid., 1.86.

54. Jaffe, *Thucydides on the Outbreak of War*, 137.

55. Bagnall, *The Peloponnesian War*, 126.

56. Kagan, *On the Origins of War and the Preservation of Peace*, 42–43.

57. Thuc. 1.75 (W).

58. Thuc. V.84–116 and VI.83.

59. Kagan, *On the Origins of War and the Preservation of Peace*, 42.

60. Thuc. 1.36 (W).
61. Kagan, *On the Origins of War and the Preservation of Peace*, 45.
62. Thuc. 1.45 (W).
63. Ibid.
64. Kagan, *On the Origins of War and the Preservation of Peace*, 46.
65. Ibid., 106.
66. Thuc. I.140 (W).
67. Ibid., 4.59.
68. Ibid., 4.62.
69. Ibid., 6.1.
70. Thuc. V.91–105.

CHAPTER 4

ALLIES, ALIGNMENTS, AND THE NATURE OF WAR

"No one is forced into war by ignorance, nor, if he thinks he will gain from it, is he kept out of it by fear."[1]

—Thucydides

"Exiled Thucydides knew
All that a speech can say
About Democracy,
And what dictators do,
The elderly rubbish they talk
To an apathetic grave;
Analysed all in his book,
The enlightenment driven away,
The habit-forming pain,
Mismanagement and grief:
We must suffer them all again."[2]

—W.H. Auden

For all the varied interpretations and attributions as philosophy, literature, tragedy, and political theory, *The History* is primarily the account of a war. Modern observers have often reduced the nature of the struggle to one between a land power (Sparta) and a sea power (Athens). Seeing the war through this myopic lens is an oversimplification common to both practitioners[3] and academics.[4] Such a characterization ignores the significant land resources of Athens, and, more significantly, the fact that Sparta's ultimate victory was a result of its matching and defeating the sea power of Athens.[5]

Consistent with the claim that the war was a conflict fought between a land power and sea power, both Gilpin and Hanson describe Sparta as "landlocked."[6] Strictly speaking, as a metropolitan area, neither Athens nor Sparta had direct access to the sea. Through the Piraeus, Athens obviously established maritime power. Sparta also had access to the sea, maintained a small fleet, and had its own dockyards for ship building. Sparta's dockyards, for example, are attested in one account celebrating the success of an Athenian general in setting "fire to the dockyards of the Lacedaemonians."[7]

Thucydides, of course, did not present the conflict in such simplistic terms. But he did provide evidence for several key elements that help us make sense of the war beyond this facile simplification. When examined, these elements can, in turn, demonstrate utility in how we analyze conflict beyond the Peloponnesian War. Building on our analysis in the previous two chapters, we argue here that contrary to conventional wisdom, the war was not simply a conflict between Spartan land power and Athenian sea power. It was also not a contest exclusively between Sparta and Athens, nor was it a single, continuous struggle. Arguing that the war was not a unitary conflict is critical, as it challenges Thucydides's own interpretation of events. Thucydides makes a forceful effort to depict the period between 431 and 404 as part of a *single*, unbroken war between Athens and Sparta.[8] His own account, however, challenges this narrative in significant ways. In his book, we see distinct phases in the war and a variety of combatants. Opening the aperture beyond Athens and Sparta—beyond the contest of sea power and land power —shows us the fundamental connections between war and policy that

Thucydides attempts to draw. Anticipating Clausewitz, Thucydides shows how politics and war can exist in tandem, with each serving and not necessarily replacing the other.

Our second fundamental argument is that a key feature of these separate phases, and of the broader conflict between Athens and Sparta, was the realignment of various actors to suit their interests. Neutrals entered the conflict and allies realigned their positions. These developments were critical to the course of the war and help us understand both the war's origins and conduct more thoroughly. These realignments were influenced by the movement of both domestic and international politics in tandem. Whereas domestic politics is a central focus in chapter 5, the conflict of opposing views on foreign policy and its ability to influence diplomatic configurations will be addressed here.

To illustrate these arguments in detail, this chapter will analyze the period between the Peace of Nicias (422–421) and the launching of the Sicilian expedition (415). This period is the part of Thucydides's work least analyzed by modern scholars. We begin with an analysis of the conditions that led Athens and Sparta to agree to peace in 422–421 and the Athenian-Spartan alliance that followed it. These agreements, which represented a triumph for the respective "peace parties" in Athens and Sparta, immediately created friction between Sparta and several of its allies. We proceed with exploring how those grievances among Sparta's allies and within the Athenian "war party" brought about diplomatic realignments that aimed to reignite the conflict. Corinth temporarily abandoned its alliance with Sparta and made an alliance with Sparta's traditional enemy, Argos. Athens, in spite of its new alliance with Sparta, then entered this clearly anti-Spartan coalition in league with Corinth and Argos. This episode, which culminated in the Spartan victory at the battle of Mantinea (418), is one of great significance.

In spite of this period's importance to the overall narrative, and the broader lessons it elucidates about international relations, it receives little attention from scholars. Thucydides himself does not deploy his greatest energy in describing this period, no doubt contributing to the shortage of modern scholarship. A partial explanation could be that the tenuous peace he describes broke down only in part. In spite of numerous problems and provocations, Sparta refused to directly renew the war against Athens during this period. Thucydides, like subsequent historians, had to grapple with these fundamental ambiguities. In many ways, the events of 422–415 did not fit Thucydides's interpretation of the conflict as a single war. Nevertheless, there is an impression of superficiality to Thucydides's account of this period, which has led some scholars to argue that the section is incomplete.

Modern classicists argue, "justifiably," that the inconsistencies and absence of information or explanation in Book 5 "betray lack of revision" on the part of Thucydides.[9] Because of the challenges inherent in examining Book 5, many historians have simply ignored the vicissitudes of this period, regarding them to be "obscure, confusing, and tedious."[10] Thucydides's treats the complex events of this period summarily. His lack of detail has made it challenging for subsequent IR scholars to derive lessons from the period. Many scholars have simply avoided the period as a result. In spite of these perceived and actual limitations, the events laid out in Thucydides's narrative nevertheless confirm his broader lessons about the fragility of power and the fundamental flexibility of alliances.

War and Peace: The Continuation of Politics at Home and Abroad

Thucydides anticipates Clausewitz's claim that war is very much the continuation of politics. He fleshes out this proposition through his case study of the war between Athens and Sparta. Defining war as a continuation of politics is often presented in the superficial sense that war continues where politics leaves off; violent clashes, therefore, replace political disputes and negotiation. Thucydides, like Clausewitz, presents a reality in which politics continues in tandem with violence. Neither politics nor diplomacy stopped with the outbreak of war between Athens and Sparta. It is important to emphasize that the continuation of politics is both domestic and international. In spite of the outbreak of war, domestic parties favoring peace continued their efforts in both Sparta and Athens, achieving a precarious success in 422–421. International diplomacy also continued vigorously. Different *poleis* put out peace feelers, reoriented (or threatened to reorient) their alignments in order to achieve their foreign-policy goals and bid to gain the support of neutral players. Changes of policy by different *poleis* influenced the outbreak of war, the course of the war, and even the war's final peace terms.

In chapters 2 and 3 we explored how the Corinthian threat to leave Sparta's Peloponnesian League spurred Sparta to defend its position as hegemon and declare war on Athens. System-level changes to the balance of power did have a role in the outbreak of war. But that role was not, as in the traditional narrative, simply the rise of Athens and its effect of Spartan fear. Instead, it was the threat of allies abandoning Sparta for neutrality or other compacts that created fear in Sparta. This fear, coupled with Sparta's awareness that its security relied on domestic stability, compelled it to fight Athens in 431. It was for the same considerations of domestic order and stability that Sparta made peace with Athens a decade later.

As Thucydides records, the first phase of the war had not gone according to plan for the Spartans, who:

> found the war had gone very differently from what they had imagined when they believed that they could destroy the power of Athens in a few years simply by laying waste her land. The disaster suffered on the island [Sphacteria] had been something which had never been known before in Sparta; her territory was being raided from Pylos...the helots were deserting, and there was always the fear that even those who remained loyal might gain confidence from the others and take advantage of the situation to make a revolution... It happened, too, that the thirty years' truce between Sparta and Argos was on the point of expiring... They

also suspected that some of the states in the Peloponnese had the intention of going over to Argos, as indeed they did.[11]

Thucydides offers a great deal in this single paragraph. First, he identifies the error of Spartan military commanders in assuming that it would be possible to achieve a quick victory by devastating Athenian territory in Attica. This tactic had failed as the Spartan king Archidamus had foreseen.[12] Older Spartans who had fought the First Peloponnesian War would have recalled its lessons as well. These men, probably skeptical about war with Athens from their experience, likely dominated the assembly of older Spartan citizens, the *Gerousia*.[13] Thucydides identifies four other sources of Spartan vulnerability at this time: the capture of one hundred and twenty *homoioi* (peers) at Sphacteria (and its concomitant blow to Spartan prestige), the desertion of large numbers of helots, the potential end of Argive neutrality, and the defection of other states in the Peloponnese, from Sparta to Argos. These factors made the Spartans particularly vulnerable and strengthened the hand of the peace party.

A push for peace, however, ran against the interests of Sparta's allies. Most prominent among them were the Corinthians. They opposed the peace on the simple basis that, from their perspective, the war had achieved none of their objectives.[14] It was Sparta's allies, Corinth most prominent among them, that had been most concerned with Athenian expansion. The war had been their attempt to curtail the power of Athens, as they had done in the First Peloponnesian War. The treaty concluded in 421 undermined this objective, and so it was viewed unfavorably by Sparta's allies. As Thucydides tells us: "After the peace treaty and the alliance... Sparta found herself immediately in fresh trouble with her allies."[15] This was a price Sparta was willing to pay, but the risks posed to its position in the Peloponnesian League were real. As we will explore presently, realignments by allies away from Sparta, and the entrance of neutrals into the conflict, soon pushed Sparta to its limits, demonstrating the vital connection between Sparta's dominance of the Peloponnesian League and the survival of its domestic political order.

Domestic politics in Athens and Sparta were reinvigorated by the military losses and setbacks suffered between 425 and 422. In both *poleis*, the "peace" parties used these losses to assert a position of ascendancy in 422. As Thucydides shows, there were tangible domestic and foreign policy reasons for a peace agreement among both the Athenians and the Spartans. With one hundred and twenty *homoioi* in Athenian hands, their most belligerent commander, Brasidas, dead in battle, and their home front vulnerable to Athenian raids, Sparta's "peace party" was able to make the case for an end to hostilities. Sparta's "peace party" was strengthened by the fact that both Spartan kings favored peace along the lines of the "dual hegemony" proposed before the outbreak of the war. King Pleistoanax, newly restored to the throne, was eager for a period of peace and calm in which no "disasters" would occur that could be used against him politically.[16] These pro-peace tendencies were reflected in Thucydides's implied argument that Sparta's citizen assembly elected a less hawkish board of ephors at this time.[17]

Like Sparta, Athens had genuine reasons to make peace. Its leading hawk, Cleon, was also dead, killed in the same battle as Brasidas. After the plague and defeat on the battlefield (particularly at Delium and Amphipolis), the Athenians "no longer possessed the same confidence in their strength that had induced them to reject previous offers of peace... They were also apprehensive about their allies, fearing that they might be encouraged by these defeats to revolt."[18] The leading political figure in Athens at this time was Nicias, a wealthy member of the elite who had performed well as a *strategos*. Like King Pleistoanax, Nicias viewed peace as the best way to avoid the vicissitudes of fortune brought out by war.[19] His goal was to lead Athens through a time of peace and recovery.

Seizing the moment, the pro-peace leaders concluded a treaty in 422-421. It was designed not only to end the war but also to provide a foundation for a lasting peace between Athens and Sparta. Its duration was set for fifty years, during which time the two sides were prohibited from taking up arms against each other or their respective allies. The

Spartans would return the city of Amphipolis in the north as well as Panactum to the Athenians; the Athenians would return five small cities taken from the Spartans. The tribute lists of the Delian League were confirmed. Both sides agreed to return all their prisoners, with the one hundred and twenty *homoioi* captured on Sphacteria being of particular importance to the Spartans. When word reached the Spartans that Argos had refused to renew their treaty, the Spartans promptly added a formal alliance with Athens to the existing peace treaty between them. Under the terms of this additional agreement, the two sides pledged to come to each other's aid in the event of invasion, to punish any invaders jointly, and to act as allies for fifty years. In a move that was as comprehensive as it was sudden, Athens and Sparta had apparently altered the political landscape of the Hellenic world.

The terms of the agreements were largely advantageous to Athens. They reflected the reality that Athens had consistently frustrated Spartan attempts to break its power, particularly control of its empire during the war. By the terms laid out in the agreements, it appeared that Athens had largely won the war: it maintained its empire, maintained its tribute revenues and suffered no territorial losses from its position *antebellum*. Sparta, now an ally, legitimized and even partnered with the Athenian empire.

Other sources confirm Thucydides's view that the Athenian public was also ready for peace. In 421, Aristophanes's play *Peace* joyously celebrated the Peace of Nicias, while skewering the tradesmen who had profited from the war and (perhaps indecently) excoriating the hawkish Cleon even though he had recently died at the Battle of Amphipolis (422). Even slightly belligerent Athenians might be convinced to end the war on these advantageous terms.

The Spartans, too, had reason to be contented. "[I]n spite of the loss of prestige she had suffered at Pylos, she emerged from the war practically unscathed, and she was still the dominant land power" in the Hellenic world.[20] This dominance, however, was put at risk by the peace. This was because Sparta's relief was not shared by its allies. These allies threatened to move away from Spartan influence, an act that would undermine the Spartan dominance that the peace was meant to preserve. These allies were the real losers of the peace, "and it was their resentment that was to cause great difficulty. The trouble started with Corinth, which had lost more than any of Sparta's allies and, feeling injured, now looked for a powerful ally who was prepared to end Spartan hegemony, to pursue Peloponnesian interests, and to assume the leadership of a new alliance."[21]

These disgruntled allies would attempt to take advantage of the recrudescent elements of the war party in Sparta in an attempt to undermine the peace. Brasidas's successor in the north, Clearidas, for example, refused to honor the terms of the treaty. Specifically, he refused to "give up Amphipolis" to the Athenians.[22] Clearidas's refusal is partially explained by his role in the Spartan victory at Amphipolis and his unwillingness to see his successes in the north (which had probably given him clients and potential or realized wealth) abandoned. His opposition to the treaty was echoed by many of Sparta's allies, but these opponents were overridden by the Spartans who "dismissed their representatives and proceeded to form an alliance with Athens."[23]

Given the feelings against the treaty both at home and abroad, its foundations were shaky. This allowed Thucydides to dismiss the significance of the Peace of Nicias in his account. "One has only to look at the facts," he notes, in some of his most argumentative tones, "to see that it is hardly possible to use the word 'peace' of a situation in which neither side gave back or received what had been promised; and part from this there were breaches of the treaty on both sides."[24] This is a post-facto justification by Thucydides to support his view of the war as a single struggle. We should not assume that the treaty was doomed to failure or that the peace parties in the respective *poleis* did not have genuine motives in finding and keeping a durable agreement. It carried with it the full force of law and oaths and was supported by important political leaders in both Athens and Sparta.

The continuation of domestic politics during this period was not confined to Athens and Sparta. In Argos, as its peace treaty with Sparta expired, there was intense competition between oligarchs and democrats for control of the *polis*. The oligarchic party favored an accommodation with Sparta through a continuation of the expiring peace. The democrats favored confrontation with Sparta and alignment with Athens. Argos is a key example of how domestic politics permeated and underpinned the continuation of foreign policy as well. Athens, Sparta, and Corinth all realized that the divisions within Argos represented a potential opening through which to realize their own foreign policy objectives.

Argive instability, combined with the actions of Clearidas, provided a key opportunity for Athenians who sought to overturn the peace before the dust had cleared from the inscriptions carrying its terms. With the death of Cleon, the "war party" in Athens was now under the control of the ambitious young aristocrat Alcibiades. Thucydides records that this party "began to make itself felt immediately" after the agreement was reached.[25] Alcibiades's opportunistic diplomatic goal was to form an alliance with Argive democrats to provoke Sparta by further weakening its position in the Peloponnese. His goal was not to live at peace under the terms of the "dual hegemony" but to bring Athens to a position of complete dominance within the Hellenic world.

Alcibiades was now one of the leading figures in Athens. A pure-bred member of the elite, he was extremely wealthy, a protégé of Pericles, and an intimate of the philosopher Socrates, who had supposedly saved his life at the battle of Delium. Alcibiades approached politics in a profoundly egotistical way. Command was a tool for personal aggrandizement. Any action that marginalized his influence on events was considered a personal insult.[26] His goal appears to have been nothing less than the undying esteem of posterity and a place among the pantheon of heroes.[27] Even in the individualistic and elite-driven politics of Athens, his manner rubbed many leading Athenians, including the famous Nicias, the wrong way.

The Spartans seem to have been aware of these overtures on behalf of Athenian hawks within Argos, and their peace party looked to engineer an alliance with Argive oligarchs as a countermeasure. This would keep Argos on the sidelines and leave Athens no chance to provoke a rupture in the peace. Corinthian diplomats, on the other hand, worked to make the peace agreement fail and push Sparta back into the fray. They also began to look toward Argos as a means to achieve this goal, hoping to establish a new Argive-Corinthian axis to dominate the Peloponnese and sideline Sparta.

From the Spartan perspective, this Argive-Corinthian alliance represented the most damaging possible realignment.[28] It would create a direct challenge to Spartan hegemony in the Peloponnese. If successful, it would also restrict Sparta to operations within the southern Peloponnese since the Corinthians could block access to Attica and Boeotia at the isthmus. A complex series of diplomatic maneuvers followed. Thucydides's account for these proceedings is surprisingly lacking. It is possible that he did not have access to the relevant information concerning Corinthian and Argive policymaking during this period and so could shed little light on what happened. It is also likely that he simply did not have the chance to revise this particular section of *The History*.

We can attempt to piece together what occurred in general terms. When Sparta failed to conclude either an alliance with Argos or a renewal of its peace treaty, Corinth and Argos became allies. Sparta continued to pressure Corinth and its other allies to reject Argive leadership in the Peloponnese. To support their position, the Spartans even leaned on their new friends in Athens.[29] A competition of sorts began between Argos and Sparta for Athenian support. Although Sparta and Athens were recent enemies, there were still a sufficient number of Athenians who believed in the old concept of the "dual hegemony" to make debate possible.

Partially facilitated by the diplomacy of Alcibiades, Athens concluded an alliance with Argos, "a sister democracy," as Thucydides tells us. Alcibiades's diplomatic success was also not entirely without precedent.

Argos and Athens had concluded an alliance in 461 and some one thousand Argive hoplites fought alongside the Athenians against the Spartans at the Battle of Tanagra in 457.[30] The new Argive-Athenian alliance, as concluded by Alcibiades, was now quickly extended to Mantinea and Elis.[31] Elis, which controlled the northwestern Peloponnese, was a traditional Spartan ally. Like many allies in this period, however, Elis was drifting from Sparta, angered by Sparta's assistance toward the independence of one of its clients. Elis's defection was yet more evidence that Sparta's control of the Peloponnesian League was in real jeopardy during this period. Some modern historians have even claimed that the league was essentially disintegrating.[32] This new alignment, however, did not suit the Corinthians, who now executed a diplomatic volte-face. They abandoned their prospects of creating a new partnership with Argos to challenge for hegemony in the Peloponnese and returned to Sparta.[33] Corinthian hostility toward Athens and its long history of partnership with Sparta proved too strong to shake. By concluding an alliance with Athens, Argos had failed to exercise the role Corinth had hoped it would as a balancer against Athens. Instead, Argos had allied with Athens against Corinth's interests.

The new Argive-Athenian alliance was quickly put to the test. In 418, Argos refused to renew its peace treaty with Sparta. The Spartans immediately marched against Argos with, as Thucydides described it, "the finest Greek army ever raised."[34] This force was composed not only of "the Spartans in full strength," but picked men from "Arcadia, Boeotia [Thebes], Corinth" and other allied *poleis*.[35] Surprisingly, the Spartan king who commanded this force, Agis II, did not engage in a decisive and victorious battle. Instead, with the full might of the Peloponnesian League at his back, he concluded a four-month treaty with the Argives and withdrew. There is much speculation about the Spartan withdrawal, and we need not engage in that debate here. It will suffice to note that many citizens in Sparta were furious with, what they perceived to be, a cowardly display by Agis. Thucydides records that they proposed a motion to destroy his home and fine him the enormous sum of one hundred thousand drachmas.[36] This proposal was not adopted, but the Spartans did take the unprecedented move of appointing a commission of ten *homoioi* "to advise the king, without whose agreement he had no authority to withdraw from enemy land."[37] This new arrangement was soon put to the test.

Not surprising from what we have already demonstrated concerning the importance of allies to Spartan foreign policy, it was a threat from another partner that spurred the Spartans to action. Shortly after establishing this new arrangement for command, word reached the Spartans from "their friends in Tegea [a large Peloponnesian ally] indicating that, if they [the Spartans] did not come at once, Tegea would secede from Sparta to join Argos and its allies."[38] Given the recent actions of Corinth and Elis, this was no idle threat. It was also, as we have already shown, one the Spartans could not ignore. They, Thucydides tells us, "reacted with unprecedented speed, sending out a full levy of citizens and helots."[39]

This crisis was critical for both Athens and Sparta. Sparta was scrambling to prevent the dissolution of the Peloponnesian League. As Spartan forces approached Argos once more, however, the Athenians were confronted with a dilemma. Their new ally, Argos, was under attack, and their treaty obligations required them to assist. But the attacker was Sparta, another Athenian ally. Most importantly, many Athenians had no wish to resume war with Sparta so soon after bringing hostilities to a close. As at Sybota fifteen years earlier, the Athenians, though small in numbers and cautious about their treaty commitments, entered the fray.

The Spartan army met the Argive and Athenian forces at Mantinea (418). In a hard-fought battle, the Athenian-Argive alliance was defeated by the Spartans and its Peloponnesian allies. Tegea remained loyal to Sparta. Only one thousand of the eight thousand hoplites in the allied army had been Athenians.[40] The Athenians could claim, with lawyerly precision, that they had only fought at Mantinea against Sparta to fulfill their treaty commitments to the Argives. Sparta had attacked Argos, an Athenian ally, and the Athenians had been obliged to defend its ally.

Under this interpretation, they had not violated their peace treaty with Sparta in spite of the fact that they had fought Spartan forces in the field. Few people, least of all Thucydides, was fooled by this legalistic approach, but the Spartans were not ready to renew the war with Athens so soon. Incredibly, the Spartans appear to have accepted a circumscribed, literal interpretation of the agreements with Athens and did not declare that Athens had violated the terms of the Peace of Nicias. Instead, with Tegea secured, Argos defeated (once more), and the loyalty of the major players in the Peloponnesian League reestablished, Spartan forces returned home.

An analysis of this complex period confirms the fluidity of alliances in the ancient Greek world. Sparta's most powerful ally, Corinth, had abandoned it and concluded an alliance with its oldest foe, Argos. Argos, a powerful neutral noted for its historic antagonism towards Sparta, had come off the sidelines in attempt to win Peloponnesian hegemony for itself, in concert with Athens. Elis, a long-standing Spartan ally, had abandoned the Peloponnesian League in favor of an alliance with Argos. Tegea, one of Sparta's closest allies, had drawn an immediate and strong reaction of Spartan support when it too threatened to leave the Peloponnesian League in favor of the new Argive-Athenian alliance. Athens, at war with Sparta for a decade, had made peace with Sparta. Athens had then allied with Sparta, before duplicitously allying with Argos almost simultaneously. In this capacity as an Argive ally, Athenian forces took the field at Mantinea against Sparta. These actions broke the spirit, if not the letter, of the peace. It is a strong indication of Sparta's continued desire for peace and its unwillingness to resume the armed conflict with Athens that it did not declare the terms of the Peace of Nicias broken by Athenian participation in the battle of Mantinea.

In this context, Sparta's victory at Mantinea was critical. It was, as Thucydides describes, "the greatest battle that had taken place for a very long time among the Hellenic states, and it was fought by the most renowned cities in Hellas."[41] It would prove to be the largest set-piece battle of the Peloponnesian War. With its victory, Sparta had done more than reassert its superiority in a conventional hoplite battle. It had preserved the bulk of its alliances and retrieved its position of dominance in the Peloponnese. After Mantinea, Sparta sought to consolidate its victory. Tegea was firmly back on its side. Corinth, although its army had not reached the field of Mantinea in time to participate in the battle, was once again considered a Spartan ally. Sparta's foreign policy priority was to restore a *modus vivendi* within the Peloponnese, and to achieve this some understanding had to be reached again with Argos.

Within Argos, the pro-Sparta oligarchs sought the overthrow of the Argive democracy and a return to peace with Sparta. When the Spartans offered peace and an alliance, this party carried the day, overruling even the persuasiveness of Alcibiades.[42] Argos and Sparta concluded a peace agreement and an alliance for fifty years. Argive envoys then demanded the withdrawal of Athenian forces from the fortified posts throughout the Peloponnese.[43] Athens's short-lived attempt to reshape the balance of power in the Peloponnese was over.

Through this diplomatic rigmarole, Sparta remained cautious with regard to Athens, resisting every Athenian provocation to renew the war. Instead of ensuring peace, Athens seemed emboldened to other provocations. Athenian forces plundered Spartan territories near Pylos. In 416, an Athenian expedition returned to the island of Melos. Melos was one of Sparta's few colonies, and the Athenians demanded that the Melians abandon Sparta and join their alliance. When the Melians refused, the Athenians besieged the island. At the conclusion of the siege, the Athenians massacred the inhabitants and enslaved the survivors. As these events played out, Thucydides comments, with a astonishment or scorn for Spartan inaction that: "[n]ot even after this did the Spartans renounce the treaty and make war."[44]

Sparta's procrastination probably provided support to the rhetoric of the Athenian war party to frame the situation as one in which Athenian power was in the ascendant and in which Athens should continue to act aggressively, if not directly against Sparta, at least in favor of its imperial ambitions. At Alcibiades's urging, Athenian foreign policy now focused on a new theater of operations in which to expand Athenian influence. Fatefully, the Athenians took the opportunity of a local conflict to send a new, and much larger, expedition to Sicily. Melos and Sicily are central to Thucydides's account and to modern interpretations of his work. They are the subject of chapter 5.

Notes

1. Thuc. 1.59 (W).
2. Auden, "September 1, 1939," https://poets.org/poem/september-1-1939.
3. Turner, "Address to Chicago Council Navy League."
4. Makinder, "The Geographical Pivot of History;" Gilpin, "The Theory of Hegemonic War," 599; Bagnall, *The Peloponnesian War*; Hanson, *A War Like No Other*, 6.
5. Platias and Koliopoulos, "Grand Strategies Clashing," 377–399.
6. Gilpin, "Peloponnesian War and Cold War," 34; Hanson, *A War Like No Other*, 5.
7. Aeschines 2.75 quoted in Fornara, *Archaic times to the end of the Peloponnesian War*, 83.
8. Even though Thucydides's detailed account of the war ends in 411, he does allude to the end of the war (which took place in 404) at several points.
9. Westlake, "Thucydides and the Uneasy Peace," 316.
10. Ibid., 315.
11. Thuc. 5.14 (W).
12. Thuc. 1.81.
13. The *Gerousia* was Sparta's council of elders. It had thirty members (twenty-eight elected plus the two kings). Members, except for the two kings, were over the age of sixty and elected by the broader citizen assembly by voice vote. They served for life. It debated which motions to bring before the broader assembly and served as a sort of supreme court.
14. Kagan, "Corinthian Diplomacy after the Peace of Nicias," 292.
15. Thuc. 5.25 (W).
16. Thuc. 5.17.
17. Ibid., 5.36.
18. Thuc. 5.14 (W).
19. Thuc. 5.16.
20. Bagnall, *The Peloponnesian War*, 186.
21. Ibid.
22. Thuc. 5.21 (W).
23. Ibid., 5.21.
24. Ibid., 5.26.
25. Ibid., 5.43.

26. Thuc. 5.43.
27. Ibid., 6.16.
28. Ibid., 5.30.
29. Ibid., 5.35.
30. Kelly, "Argive Foreign Policy in the Fifth Century B.C." 84–85.
31. Thuc. 5.44 (W).
32. Legon, "The Peace of Nicias," 324.
33. Thuc. 5.48.
34. Thuc. 5.60 (H).
35. Ibid.
36. Thuc. 5.64. One drachma was the daily wage paid to a rower on an Athenian trireme.
37. Thuc. 5.64 (H).
38. Ibid.
39. Ibid.
40. Corinthian forces attempted to join the battle (on the side of Sparta) but arrived too late to participate (Thuc. 5.64).
41. Thuc. 5.74 (W).
42. Thuc. 5.76.
43. Ibid., 5.80.
44. Thuc. 5.115 (W).

Chapter 5

Thucydides and Realism

A Journey from Melos to Sicily

"It is better evidence than that of the poets, who exaggerate the importance of their themes, or of the prose chroniclers, who are less interested in telling the truth than in catching the attention of their public."[1]

—Thucydides

"By the time Margaret Truman, woke up, she found her two sons perched on either side of their grandfather's (President Harry S. Truman) chair. "Neither of us was moving while he read to us from a book that didn't have any pictures in it," Daniel recalled. "And she said, 'What in God's name are you reading to those children?' And he showed her. It was Thucydides. 'The History of the Peloponnesian War.' At 6 o'clock in the morning. To a 4-year-old and a 2-year old."[2]

—Clifton Truman Daniel

CUTING AND PASTING HISTORY

Wake any political scientist from a dead sleep with the words, "[T]he strong do what they can" and they will likely finish the sentence, "the weak suffer what they must."[3] Perhaps no sentence in Thucydides's work is more enduring or foundational to IR theory, presenting, as it supposedly does, a microcosm of realism writ large. In this chapter, we will explore the Melian Dialogue (Book 5.84–116) and the Sicilian expedition. While the Melian Dialogue receives enormous attention in the existing scholarship about Thucydides, both historical and theoretical, the dynamics of the Sicilian expedition are considered in detail less often. In our view, however, they are inherently linked and must be understood in relation to each other. When taken together, they provide powerful insights into the debates of "realism" present in Thucydides as well as his ability to blend domestic politics and foreign policy. The strong not only do what they want but also must consider that in doing what they want, they may suffer what they must as well. International politics, as we see in Thucydides (and as argued in liberalism), is iterative and interactive. These factors should recommend limits, rather than the untrammeled exercise of power in the name of self-interest. As we argue throughout this book, each episode can only be understood if we look at its broader context both within Thucydides and beyond. In this particular instance, it is also necessary to challenge not only our interpretations of Thucydides but also the evidence that Thucydides offers.

Thucydides's realism, as derived from the Melian Dialogue, has become both foundational and contentious. This chapter will not seek to solve this fundamental debate in IR theory, although we will engage with some of its contributions. Instead, our primary goal is to offer some deeper perspectives on the particular episode of Melos that are often left out of many of the theoretical debates. It is our goal to deepen and inform this important theoretical debate by considering the broader evidence. We argue that four critical factors defined the Melian Dialogue—factors that are often forgotten when the dialogue is approached as a discrete episode: 1) Athenian forces arrived at Melos during the tenuous Peace of Nicias, after the defeat of Athenian forces at the Battle of Mantinea. Officially, however, there was no state of war with Sparta. 2) The Melians were not pacific neutrals but were a tribute-paying client of Sparta. They had even fought against the Athenians before. 3) Thucydides hints at political divisions within Melos that the Athenians, in all likelihood, eventually exploited in order to take the city. The Melians were not overwhelmed by Athenian power *per se* but were actually defeated by treachery from "within." 4) Melos was not a random, tiny island, but a strategically located *polis* of sufficient size to have strategic impact.

There are also misconceptions about the Athenian expedition to Sicily. First, although the expedition represented aspects of Athenian imperialism and opportunism, the Athenian campaign against Syracuse in 415 was also undertaken in response to two existing alliances: with Egesta and Leontini. The campaign of 415 was also not Athens's first foray into Sicily but the latest in a series of operations on the island. Contrary to the picture painted by Thucydides, in which the Athenians went blindly to their eventual destruction, earlier expeditions in Sicily had been reasonably successful and had provided the Athenians with knowledge about the island. Finally, Athens was familiar with the dynamics of significant foreign campaigns (and even foreign defeats), having launched a massive operation in Egypt between 460 and 455, during the First Peloponnesian War. This was a major failure, as Thucydides records, but hardly deterred Athens from taking similar risks in its foreign policy.[4]

Thucydides's account of the tragic events in Melos and Sicily does reinforce some principles of realism. There are examples of balancing and bandwagoning. States seek to maximize their power. Alliances are formed and leveraged to optimize security. In second-hand accounts, the Melian Dialogue is often depicted as a stark clash between realism and liberalism, with realism the clear winner.[5] While the student of international politics sees the general array of realist variables, they student is still left with the question of which variant of realism is most supported and how it should be applied. Is it classical realism or neo-realism, offensive realism or defensive realism? Is structure the key determinant of choice and outcome?

For decades, scholars have recognized these ambiguities and fought against oversimplification from this case, arguing that the Athenian conquest of Melos offers us far more than just a confirmation of refutation of realism. The importance of this scholarly debate is reinforced by the unique and profound elements of the dialogue itself. First, Thucydides departs from his usual practice of recording speech and counter-speech to present the discussions in Melos. The exchange between the Athenians and Melians is the only dialogue in his book. This approach, which anticipates the dialogues of Plato, "underlines the distinctly 'philosophical' argument development by the Athenians."[6] The significance of the passage is further reinforced by the discontinuity between the episode's size within Thucydides's work and its strategic significance. The dialogue itself is "quite substantial" while the fate of Melos is generally considered to have had a "negligible importance for the course" of the war.[7] That the episode was of "negligible importance for the course" of the war is itself debatable; but the significance of this particular campaign should not be confused with the very real strategic significance of the island of Melos itself.

One reason for the philosophical importance of the dialogue is the fact that Thucydides infuses the exchange with critical issues such as the meaning of justice and the apposition of justice to power and expediency. The dialogue has even been interpreted as symbolic of Thucydides's view of a turning point for the Athenian imperial project and of the "clash… of opposite philosophies and ways of life" in which the "independence of Melos represents the last survival of *polis* autonomy in the Aegean."[8] These facets make the dialogue seminal to Thucydides's work and highly challenging to interpret.

As a result, we see interpretations along a wide range. Garst argues that instead of straightforward support for realism, Thucydides's work should be treated "as a contested terrain for realist and critical approaches to international relations theory."[9] This is certainly a fair point. Clark goes further, arguing that asserting the behavior of the weak and the strong as a "law outside the context of the Melian dialogue is not to exploit a general principle, but to initiate an open-ended exercise in question-begging."[10]

These enduring debates are sustained by the ambiguities within *The History* and by the inherent richness of Thucydides's work.

As with all of Thucydides's work, the meanings within the Melian Dialogue are obscured when readers interpret events as if they were self-contained and critical lines as if they represented Thucydides's own conclusion. Interpretations of the Melian Dialogue are emblematic of this problem. Should we interpret the mantra that strong do what they can and the weak suffer what they must as a deeply held belief of Thucydides? Or, is it merely something recorded by Thucydides, reflecting what the Athenian emissaries to Melos said? Modern scholars have been quick to wade into this debate. While some believe "that the views expressed by the Athenians at Melos are on the whole thoroughly consistent" with those of Thucydides,[11] many have argued instead that "Thucydides's history has the form and meaning of a tragic drama in which Athenian hubris, exemplified by Athens's behavior at Melos, is properly punished at Sicily."[12]

How these two contradictory views fit into Thucydides's realism remains a challenge to scholars. Doyle tries to reconcile them, arguing that the Melian Dialogue does support basic claims about Thucydides's realist view of the world, but that it is also evidence of "continuity" rather than "unity" between Thucydides and realism as we understand it today.[13] In his view, Thucydides does not "endorse the untrammeled pursuit of 'might makes right.'"[14] Others have taken this further, arguing that the treatment of Melos was an "enduring black stain on Athenian history."[15] Rather than recommending the callous calculations of realism, "Thucydides regarded the crude exercise of power [in Melos and Sicily] as pathological, as something to be shunned, not emulated."[16] In this interpretation, "the Athenian defeat in Sicily is the strategic lesson of the massacre at Melos."[17] It symbolizes the pride before the fall. In Sicily, "the Athenians, in their hubris, go too far and begin their own eventual destruction."[18] Yet, as some scholars do notice, the Athenian behavior in Melos had certain parallels with the atrocity carried out by the Spartans at Plataea in 427.[19] Both Thucydides and modern scholars seem unconvinced that this represented a decay of Spartan political culture, constituted a "black stain" on Sparta's reputation, or set Sparta on a path to its eventual downfall. So we are, in a sense, forced back to square one when confronting the case of Melos.

If the functions of theory are to describe, explain, predict, and prescribe, does Thucydides's presentation of realism manage to do all four? Clearly, he describes the tenets of realism, though they are not labeled as such. Even when he does not attempt to explain directly in his own analysis, the evidence he presents and the cases he recounts can be used to build credible explanations. But are his predictions consistent with what a structural level of analysis claims to offer? Alliances, for example, are an important tool for realists, but did alliances like the Delian League in its many variations reflect the power of the largest, most conventionally powerful state? What value is an alliance to a powerful state when smaller states can openly or deceitfully prod, constrain, and manipulate that larger state to its ends, as when the Egestaeans help convince the Athenians to campaign against Syracuse? If his use of realism does not prove adequately predictive, how can scholars, pundits, and policymakers reliably prescribe optimal policy choices?

Ultimately, a richer reading of Thucydides with full regard for the context he provides demonstrates that realism is one of several levels of analysis used to explore this period in the Peloponnesian War. Domestic politics played a very significant role in the policy choices made by the states in the Greek world. Public opinion (at least that of the elites) mattered, even in states with no recognizable democratic process. Inconsistent with the desire of realists to see states as unified actors, there were clear divisions evident in Thucydides's constant recounting of debates. As a result, internal political coalitions formed, clashed, and struggled for dominance or consensus. Agenda setting and bargaining were constant, consequential processes within states.

The standard operating procedures of governments and their constituent agencies forced and constrained decisions and directly affected outcomes. This was true in the details of basic administration of state affairs, in the budgeting of government funds, and in the complexities of raising and launching armies. Of particular note during this period were the workings of civil-military relations, particularly in an early democratic state such as Athens. At first glance, the military and the civil were one. Athenian *strategoi* (generals) were elected from the Assembly (almost always from its leading political figures), ensuring that those who set security policies would share in the risks associated with executing those policies. However, once elected, the *strategoi* were not free to act with impunity. This is also important as we consider the Athenian actions in Melos. The size and composition of military forces required authorization. Funding levels were set and fiscal management was conducted by the Assembly. Leaders in the field could not act unilaterally on the establishment and coordination of military alliances. Laws, treaties, and established norms had to be followed and could not be diluted or circumvented without the Assembly's permission. Finally, strong oversight was maintained. Reports were filed through the appropriate government channels and the performance of *strategoi* was closely watched. We clearly see this process in action during the debate about the campaign in Sicily. In the event of failure, commanders faced the prospects of significant personal costs, as Thucydides's own exile demonstrates. There were even more extreme punishments. In one instance, a group of six generals, including Xanthippus, the son of Pericles, was put on trial for failing to rescue the survivors of the naval engagement at Arginusae (406). They were put on trial collectively, charged with violating the constitution, convicted, and executed. By exploring these various factors in tandem with an analysis of the Melian Dialogue and the Sicilian expedition, we can attempt to create a more substantive sense of the lessons these episodes hold.

The events Thucydides describes at the end of Book 5 were not the Melians' first clash with Athens in the course of the war. Nine years earlier, Athens had sent an expedition to Melos with more than two-thousand heavy infantry and more ships than would support the second Athenian endeavor. The Melians turned away this Athenian effort to incorporate Melos into its empire, but not before Athenian soldiers laid waste to parts of Melos before departing.[20] When the second Athenian expeditionary force arrived in Melos, there was a tenuous peace between Sparta and Athens. As a result, the Melians were at least partially surprised at the bellicose attitude of the Athenians and their peremptory demands. The peace itself was fraying to the breaking point. The Spartan response to the Athenian provocation in moving on Melos—the last island in the Aegean not incorporated within the Athenian Empire— would demonstrate its resolve to resume hostilities.

In spite of their justifiable surprise, it is inaccurate to portray the Melians as pacifists intent on isolation; they should have had few illusions that pretending neutrality would provide them security. As Thucydides noted, Melos was already in an "openly hostile stance" when Athenian forces arrived.[21] The best they could hope for was that the shaky peace treaty between Athens and Sparta would protect them or, the more unlikely option, that Sparta would consider the Athenian attack on Melos a violation of the peace and reignite the war. The Melians openly acknowledged their reliance on Sparta. The two cities had an historic and ethnic attachment. Thucydides goes so far as to declare Melos a Spartan colony, although its establishment was sufficiently in the past that Melos had developed a unique culture distinct from Sparta. Nevertheless, it was clear that Melos and Sparta were closely linked, with Melos providing tribute to Sparta during the war.[22] Given these ties and the record of recent battles between Athens and Melos, conventional concerns for security never would have been far from the minds of Melian leaders.

The dialogue came fifteen years into the war, when Athens and Sparta had formally agreed to a peace treaty.[23] Both Athens and Sparta had been worn down at home as well as on the battlefield as the costs of the long war—military, political, economic, and social—continued to mount. During the previous fifteen years, the conduct of the war had been brutal. Time and again, Thucydides concludes his account of battles and sieges by reporting the execution of all adult males on the losing side and the selling of all women and children into slavery. Entire cities were reduced to rubble, and crop fields razed. The strong, it seems, truly were doing want they wished while the weak suffered what they must. As Athenian ships appeared off the coast of Melos, the Melians were not unreasonable to believe that this pattern of slaughter and enslavement would continue, to their cost.

DIALOGUE AND DEFEAT

The Athenians's interests were more than simply taking offense at the Melians's loose interpretation of neutrality. A quick glance at a map demonstrates that Melos was located at the southwestern most of the Cycladic islands, a key spot in the Aegean. When Athens sailed its forces to the Peloponnese and beyond, their ships were particularly vulnerable as they crossed through the sea lanes between Melos and the Peloponnesian coast. As explained in chapter 3, the ability of the Athenians to sail along the coast of the Peloponnese, inflicting economic damage and inciting helot uprisings, was an essential component of its wartime strategy. It is not accurate to dismiss Melos, as some scholars have "as a tiny, neutral island... in no way strategically important."[24] In the context of the ancient Greek world, Melos was a medium-sized island,[25] aligned with Sparta, in a strategically important location controlling access to the southern and western coasts of the Peloponnese. It was important enough, for example, to merit its own inscription along with thirty other *poleis* on the famous serpent column erected at Delphi in honor of the victory at Plataea.[26]

In other words, there were real reasons for the Athenians to come to Melos with their demands. But if the strong, in fact, do what they want— and even the most basic analysis demonstrates that control of Melos was what Athens should want—they still chose not to immediately plunge into combat with the Melians. Rather than violently exercising military might, the Athenian forces first offered Melos an alternative. Furthermore, consistent with their own domestic political ideology and practice, the Athenians first asked to speak directly to the citizens of the island.

The leaders of Melos refused Athens's request. Instead, the Athenian *strategos* met with "the authorities and the privileged few."[27] This restriction is an example of the role domestic politics and ideology consistently plays in Thucydides's writing. The Melian leaders' insistence on keeping their citizens away from the Athenians mirrored the concerns of their parent *polis*, Sparta, which constantly feared contamination of its population by the tenets of Periclean broad-based democracy. Early in his book, Thucydides tells us that similar fears were already on full display in 464, during the fallout from a major earthquake in the Peloponnese, which triggered a helot uprising.[28] With the Athenian appeal on Melos limited to talks between military and political leaders, there would be no speeches with lofty rhetorical appeals to the masses. The Melians stated at the outset that they knew Athens had already set their desired outcome and that this was not a genuine negotiation. The Melians would have two choices—win the "moral argument" and face war or accept the arguments of the Athenians and "face servitude."[29] By "servitude," the Melians meant their forced acquiescence to membership within the Athenian Empire and their reduction to the status of tribute-paying vassal.

For their part, the Athenians conceded that it would do them no good to pad their argument with platitudes about their role in defeating Persia. Such a defense would amount to no more than "a great mass of words that nobody would believe."[30] In return, they expected Melos to agree to join their empire. The Melians should not state that they bore no hostility toward Athens. The Athenians declared that they would both be direct in their assertions. The acceptance of these ground rules strips away the characterization of Melos as the representatives of a pure and just neutrality. Likewise, Athens's initiative to negotiate softens the traditional harsh depiction of Athens as merciless brutes. The Athenians came to Melos with the clear political goal of bringing Melos into their empire or, failing that, to destroy them as a potential enemy.

Despite this candor and the increasing unlikelihood of Melos conceding, the Athenians continued to press their case for a peaceful resolution. Why did they not cease the pretense of peace talks and launch an attack? The Athenian insistence on meeting with the Melians is only one instance of appealing for settlement before resorting to force. While the Peloponnesian War is best known for its conflict and violence, there are numerous other examples of diplomacy within Thucydides's account that warrant study. Such study reveals that diplomacy and war did not hand off one to the other in a sharply delineated sequence of diplomacy-stop-war-stop-diplomacy. They are constantly intermingled and often interdependent.

The relationships between governments were shaped, constrained, and propelled by treaties, alliances, and ongoing diplomacy. The debates and discussions between city-states were as important as those within. The city-states of the Greek world took diplomatic exchanges and treaty obligations seriously. When a state agreed to a treaty, the leaders publicly swore to its provisions, sometimes formally memorializing the agreement with a monument bearing the terms inscribed in stone along with the names of the representatives from each *polis* who solemnly swore oaths to uphold its provisions. Deciding when and how to terminate an armistice or to ignore a call to defend an ally involved considerable political deliberation and the potential for moral and even religious outrage.

This is all highlighted by a significant complicating factor affecting the behavior of Athens, Sparta, and Melos at the time of the Melian Dialogue. In 421, a treaty had halted the war between Sparta and Athens. The resulting agreements, the Peace of Nicias and the Athenian-Spartan alliance, were meant to last for fifty years. From the start, there were assertions that the treaty had already been broken, but no one seemed willing to be the first to act as if the treaty was null.[31] In this way, the treaty may have been a factor in why Sparta ultimately did not come to Melos's aid. It could also have been the reason why Athens felt free to attack Melos without the fear of (immediate) Spartan intervention.

The discussion between the Athenians and the Melians began with the Athenians clearly holding the advantage. Still, they offered the Melians an alternative to destruction. How burdensome the tribute tax and how restrictive the feared servitude are not clear. If we can take the other member states of the Athenian Empire as examples, the tribute would probably not have been ruinous to the people of Melos. From the tribute list of 454/3, we know that Athenian clients were required to pay 1/60 of their revenues to the Athenian treasury.[32] Although we know nothing about their respective economies and prosperity, Samothrace, a slightly larger island than Melos, appears on the list from 454/3 and paid 600 drachma in the year's assessment.[33] For context, a skilled workman or hoplite could earn one drachma a day during this period.[34] During the war, the assessments were increased, and Thucydides tells us that after the disaster in Sicily, the Athenians scrapped the tribute system altogether and replaced it with a five percent tax on each of their clients in order to increase revenues.[35]

This evidence suggests that the cost was not financially prohibitive, but the Melians would have sacrificed the treasured Greek *eleutheria*—the political autonomy that defined free *poleis* across the Hellenic world. Many states had made this concession; some regretted it. The Melians would certainly have had enough evidence from recent history to believe that submitting to Athens would not require an excessive financial price. Besides, it is important to remember that they were already paying tribute to Sparta. Were the Athenians asking for so much more than what Melos was already giving Sparta? Were they demanding Melos join in an attack on Sparta? Was there a requirement for Melos to adopt the Athenian model of democracy? What was the actual cost that Melos feared? Could it possibly have exceeded military defeat and slaughter? Did the elites fear for their own position more than they feared for the nation's survival? It is this last point, hinting at internal divisions, that provides a potentially convincing explanation for the Melians' choices. The cost to Melos was not economic but political, and the political cost was the removal of its oligarchic government and its replacement with a broader form of democracy. A highly likely scenario, given what we know of the dynamics of this period, was that there was a degree of *stasis* (civil strife) on Melos, common to the Hellenic world. This hypothesis is supported by the Melian refusal to allow the Athenians to speak to the broader populace and the concurrent struggle between oligarchs and democrats in Argos. These dynamics also had a precedent in the recent struggles in Argos, described prior to the affair of Melos in Book 5. In the very sentence before Thucydides recounts the Athenian expedition against Melos, he records that "Alcibiades took a fleet of twenty ships to Argos and arrested those Argives who were still thought suspect and sympathetic to Sparta—three hundred men, whom the Athenians then deposited in neighboring islands under their control."[36] These must have been supporters of Argos's short-lived oligarchic regime. There was also a precedent for *stasis* between oligarchs and democrats in the case of Mytilene where "the oligarchs had led the rebellion while the demos remained sympathetic to Athens."[37] These contemporary events suggest that Melian oligarchs sought to maintain their cooperation with Sparta, while democratic elements sought to capitulate, establish a democratic regime in Melos, and throw in their lot with Athens.

In response to the Athenian demands, the Melians provided an argument based on the principle of neutrality. They reinforced this with warnings to the Athenians of the repercussions of being labeled an unjust conqueror. Athens, weary from more than a decade at war, did not accept these arguments but still offered an option for survival. The Melians, like numerous other Greek *poleis*, would have to surrender their political autonomy and join the Athenian alliance as a tribute paying member.

The Melians would still not accept the Athenian argument. In the course of appealing for their continued autonomy, they pointed to a grim future for Athens if it continued on this course of aggression. Oppressed *poleis* within the Athenian Empire, argued the Melians, would eventually rise up and treat Athens as Athens had been treated so many of its foes. Taking Melos, whether through capitulation to demands or through battlefield defeat, would ultimately make Athens weaker. Melian resistance was not suicidal. Both the Melians and the Athenians were well aware of the fundamental challenges inherent in siege warfare. During this period, sieges were often both long and expensive. At Potidaea, for example, four thousand six hundred hoplites were deployed for more than three years of operations, at a cost of more than one thousand talents per year. This demonstrated both the expenditure and potential duration common in siege warfare even when a great power like Athens attacked a small *polis*. The Athenians were not moved either by Melian speculation about the end of Athens's empire or by the potential cost of laying siege to Melos. They remained confident in their power and focused on the demands of the present.

Did the Melians fully believe their own arguments? Could they not sacrifice their stated principles of autonomy? Were they willing to accept extermination? Or did they fully expect that Sparta would arrive in time to save them? Were they confident that they could frustrate the Athenian siege? No record of the policy deliberations in Melos has survived and neither Thucydides nor subsequent historians make any speculation as to their internal debate. We can piece together the few clues found in this second-hand account of their exchange with Athens, as we speculate about their willingness to gamble so much with so little in their favor. The oligarchs in Melos were undoubtedly concerned with their own survival and were willing to risk the security of the *polis* itself in order to shield themselves. Their best hopes for survival were the potential for Spartan help and the fundamental difficulties of siege warfare. They did not shrink from battle and when efforts to talk the Athenians out of conquest failed, they gave an aggressive and prolonged defense. That campaign dragged on as the Melians successfully captured portions of the Athenian siege walls. The Athenians recaptured and improved their positions, then withdrew a portion of their army and left a small siege force to continue pressuring the Melians.[38]

In the final summer of the campaign, the further fraying of the peace between Athens and Sparta offered a hope—"that comforter in danger," as Thucydides famously calls it—to the Melian defenders.[39] Athenian harassment of the Peloponnese continued, and Athenian forces "captured a great quantity of plunder," from Spartan territory. Surely in the face of these provocations, Sparta would finally renounce the treaty and attack Athens. For whatever reason, they did not. However, the Spartans did issue a proclamation asserting that other states in their alliance were free to attack the Athenians. The Peace of Nicias had essentially broken down. The Corinthians took advantage of this official authorization to settle "private quarrels" with Athens.[40] Perhaps Corinth, whose innovations in naval engineering and tactics preceded and nearly equaled that of Athens, might sail to the aid of Melos with soldiers recruited from across the Peloponnese. In the end, no one came to the Melians's aid. The known historic record does not yet reveal the demands and pleas that may have been sent from Melos to Sparta and its allies before or during the siege. Whatever those communications may have been, the Melians fought on alone. Athens was still militarily pressured by Sparta's allies on the mainland and in island campaigns throughout the Aegean. Lost in the narrow focus on events on Melos is the fact that the wider conflict was reigniting once more. The Athenians were simultaneously engaged in hostilities with several enemies on different fronts. This could have helped to relieve some of the pressure on Melos but did not.

The eventual Athenian victory does not truly answer the question of whether Athenian might ultimately made right. The Melians' defeat, writes Thucydides, was not the result of superior Athenian military power but was due to "some internal treachery." The Melians surrendered with acceptance of the terms of defeat the Athenians promised in the beginning. Under the direction of the Athenian *strategos* Philocrates (whose name ironically means "lover of power"), the men of Melos were executed.[41] The woman and children were enslaved. Athens took the island as its own and sent five hundred Athenians to establish a new colony on the ashes and graves of the defeated Melians.[42]

The identity of those who chose to defect and their reasons for doing so are not known. It is likely that the "treachery" was the work of a pro-Athenian party, likely drawn from the poorer citizens, the broader *demos*, who opposed oligarchic resistance and favored democracy. This interpretation is clearly supported by a similar pattern of behavior established during the Athenian siege of Mytilene a decade before. At Mytilene, "the common people... had no part in the revolt and once they were in possession of arms took their own decision to hand the city over to [the Athenians]."[43] Regardless of who opened the gates for the Athenians, it can be concluded that it was not Athens's superior "strength" alone that were ultimately sufficient and decisive. Furthermore, it can be said that the Athenians did offer Melos a chance to determine its own fate when they clearly had the means and motive to bypass that diplomatic nicety.

It is also worth briefly exploring the harshness of the Athenian action in Melos. The Athenians clearly came to Melos for strategic reasons but were also aware of the broader political implications of the situation. Modern scholars have been quick to contrast the (last minute and incomplete) mercy meted out by Athens in Mytilene with the total brutality of their actions in Melos. This difference is interpreted as evidence of the moral decline of Athens and its political leadership away from the ideals of Pericles.[44] But we must look beyond this shorthand. The "mercy" shown to Mytilene in 427 was incomplete, at best. Over a thousand members of the Mytilenean oligarchic faction were nevertheless executed by the Athenians. The city's walls were torn down and its ships seized. The island itself was divided into three administrative districts and was colonized by Athenians.[45] The echoes to Melos are immediate and transparent. Such realities argue for consistency in Athenian policy from Mytilene to Melos, not a rupture due to the disappearance of Periclean ethics.

For their part, the Melians were the last islanders in the Aegean outside of Athens's power and they occupied a strategic position along the route to the Peloponnese. By treating them harshly, Athens was hoping to provide a lesson in terror to intimidate other islanders who might consider rebellion.[46] As we have seen in chapter 3, one of Athens's main fears—and one of the greatest challenges to its power—was rebellion in its empire. At the same time, Athens could use Sparta's failure to come to the aid of its clients as evidence of Spartan weakness and of Spartan unreliability. Athens had already tried to undo the Peloponnesian League through its overtures to Argos and Corinth. By brutally punishing Melos, Athens put Sparta in a bind. Sparta could resume direct military operations against Athens and suffer the onus of formally "breaking" the peace, or it would demonstrate weakness by sitting idly by while its client was destroyed. Either outcome would suit the preferences of the Athenian war party.

We must also remember that, unlike the case of Mytilene which precedes Melos and the case of Sicily which follows, Thucydides does not present any debate over the actions in Melos. We cannot assume, however, that no debate took place. A lack of debate is anomalous within the context of *The History*. It could be that Thucydides does not record a debate because it does not suit the narrative of Melos representing a break with previous Athenian policy rather than a continuation of it. It is also possible that the instructions to coopt or destroy Melos had already been taken in Athens—we do not have evidence for any debate in Athens either—and that the commander on the ground had precious little discretion. Under such circumstances, the leaders of the expedition could only consider a compromise under the fear of being prosecuted in Athens upon their return for failing to implement the will of the people.

The only contemporary evidence we have to provide a critique of Athenian policy in Melos comes from the great tragic poet Euripides. His *Trojan Woman*, produced in 415, solemnly rebuked the citizens of Athens for the horrors they had meted out to the Melians through a chilling allegory with the destruction of Troy. Burning cities, dead husbands, murdered children, women raped and taken away as slaves, streets that run with blood—all these horrors meted out by the victorious Greeks were grimly paraded before the eyes of the Athenian *demos*, particularly for the archons, officials, and literary judges siting in the front row.

The play was a blatant attack but a warning too. Euripides cautioned on the perils of exercising power so nakedly. In *The Trojan Women* no less an authority than the god Poseidon warns: "A fool is he who sacks the towns of men, with shrines and tombs, the dead man's hallowed home, for at the last he makes a desert round himself, and dies."[47] We do not know how impactful such criticism was within Athenian society or how receptive Athenians were to having their atrocities so obviously paraded before their eyes. Euripides had a turbulent history with his native *polis* where he was both persecuted and admired. His controversial play won second prize at that year's Dionysian festival, runner-up to an offering from the mediocre poet Xenocles, none of whose works survive.

As we have already stated, it is wrong to conclude that the outcome of the Melian campaign is a definitive endorsement of realism as a prescription for policymakers. Book 5 ends with Athenian success at Melos. Book 6 follows with Athens setting course for the disaster in Syracuse. If read in immediate succession, the sentences that end Book 5 crash against the beginning of Book 6. After the fall of Melos, the Athenians

> put to death all the men of military age who they took, and sold the women and children as slaves. Melos itself they took over for themselves, sending out later a colony of 500 men. In the same winter the Athenians resolved to sail again against Sicily.[48]

As identified above, political scientists have commented on this apposition and see it as evidence of Thucydides's condemnation of Athenian policy on Melos. Historians have noticed it too. For Jacqueline de Romilly, the juxtaposition is certainly no accident. She emphasized how Thucydides used juxtaposition in order to establish "a coherent and comprehensible sequence."[49] So, to continue the sequence, we must follow Thucydides and turn from Melos to Sicily.

AFTERMATH AND AMBITION

As it would be for centuries to come, in Thucydides's time the island of Sicily was an important crossroads for trade, culture, migration, and warfare. In his opening paragraphs to Book 6, Thucydides recounts overlapping waves of Laestrygonians, Sincanian Iberians, Trojans, Phoenicians, Sicels, Corinthians, Chalcidians, Megarans, Rhodians, Cretans, Gelans, Messinans, Samians, Cumaens, Chalcisans, and Ionians breaking over the Sicilian shores. Some were colonists, some were settlers, some were refugees from war, and some were shipwrecked sailors and pirates. Over the centuries, they co-existed, intermarried, attacked each other, and rose up in revolt and civil war within their territories. Some, like the Syracusans who traced their origins to Corinth, maintained political ties to their communities of origin. Others had severed links with a particular state but maintained cultural identities. Still others gradually developed their own cultures and identities as new settlements emerged. Systems of governance ranged from constitutional democracies to old-fashioned tyrannies.[50]

The Athenians who set their sights on Sicily were, as Thucydides noted, "for the most part ignorant of the size of the island and of the numbers of inhabitants, both Hellenic and native, and they did not realize that they were taking on a war of almost the same magnitude as their war against the Peloponnesians."[51] Despite their lack of information, some in Athens were eager to attack. In Thucydides's account, arrogance yoked to ambition is evident throughout as a fundamental characteristic (and flaw) of the Sicilian campaign. This is undoubtedly an oversimplification and one that serves Thucydides's argument about the inferiority of Athenian leadership and political life after Pericles. Some of the Athenians who debated the campaign against Syracuse had, in fact, already campaigned in Sicily. In 427, the Athenians had sent twenty ships to Sicily to support Leontini and a coalition of Ionian Greeks against Syracuse and a coalition of Dorian *poleis*, which were all members of "the Spartan alliance." The expedition not only supported Athenian allies against Spartan allies but also, as Thucydides himself admits, served as "an experiment to see if it would be possible to bring Sicily under their control." More immediately, Thucydides also identifies the essential role Sicily played in supplying food to their Peloponnesian allies. Appeals to Ionian kinship aside, Thucydides argues that "in reality" the Athenian motivation was to "prevent any import of corn [grain] from that area to the Peloponnese."[52] From this account, we see that the internal politics, economic potential, and military capabilities of Sicily were all things of which Athenian policymakers would have had some awareness.

Those favoring the expedition were encouraged in their desires by a delegation from Egesta.[53] The Egestaeans were warring with their neighbors the Selinuntines and the Syracusans. The Egestaeans needed external support in their conflict and approached other Sicilian *poleis* and Carthage before settling on sending an embassy to Athens. The Egestaeans were not a random group coming to Athens for help in a time of crisis. A fragmentary inscription of uncertain date (458/7; 454/3; or 418/7?) from the Acropolis attests to an alliance between Athens and Egesta.[54] Athenian intervention, argued the Egestaeans, was not simply to aid Egesta in a limited, local conflict. The threat, they argued—echoing the appeal of the Corcyraeans from fifteen years earlier—was that Egesta would only be the first city subjugated by Syracuse. If Athens failed to come to the aid of Egesta, the Syracusans would subjugate them on the path to conquering the entire island of Sicily. In time, the Syracusans, Spartan allies, would be a threat to Athens itself.[55]

The Egestaeans bolstered their pleas with specific reminders of another Sicilian *polis*, Leontini. Athens had intervened almost ten years previously to help defend Leontini from Syracusan aggression. As with Egesta, Athens had a formal treaty of alliance with Leontini dating back to 433/2.[56] At Leontini, as in other cases, the Athenians had intervened on the side of the democratic party, which had been attacked by the Syracusans in order to prevent them from carrying out a policy of land redistribution.[57] Now, the Egestaeans argued, "if Syracuse, after driving out the people of Leontini, were allowed to escape scot-free, and to go on to destroying the remaining allies of Athens until she acquired compete control of Sicily, the danger would then have to be faced that at some time or other the Syracusans... would come with a large force to the aid of their Dorian kinsmen." Syracuse's "Dorian kinsmen," of course, was a veiled reference to the Dorian Spartans who were a hair's breadth away from re-launching military operations against the Athenians in the wake of the collapse of the Peace of Nicias. Moved by this argument—and, as Thucydides reports, in a desire to "see whether the money which (the Egestaeans) said was in the treasury and the temples really did exist," a delegation was sent to Egesta.[58]

As mentioned above, there were remarkable similarities between the Corcyraean embassy that launched the first phase of the war and the Egestaean embassy that reignited it. In the case of Sicily, as in the case of Corcyra, the Athenians were approached by allies, the Egestaeans. With a history of intervention in Sicily, the Athenians were easily persuaded to send another expedition, this time a larger one, with the intent of establishing Athenian control over much, if not all, of the island. Again, intervention was framed as necessary for maintaining Athenian dominance, particularly at sea, although it had the double advantage of interrupting food supplies to the Peloponnese and perhaps augmenting the supply of grain to the ever-hungry city of Athens itself. As with the case of Corcyra, the primary concern was securing Athens's empire. As in the case of Corcyra, the initial Athenian foe was not Sparta. In the Corcyraean case, the foe was Sparta's ally, Corinth. In the case of Sicily, it was Syracuse, a powerful *polis* also allied to Sparta that had a shared Dorian heritage with Sparta and was also related to Corinth. Not surprisingly, as in the crisis over Corcyra, the prospect of Athenian intervention brought with it appeals to both Corinth and Sparta for assistance against Athens. As in the earlier case, there was a debate in Sparta over whether Athenian actions constituted a violation of the existing treaty between Athens and Sparta and therefore a justification for war. Once more, it was Sparta's allies, predominantly Corinth, in the lead in opposing Athens and then in working to convince Sparta to enter the conflict. Various *poleis* in Sicily had to navigate the difficulties of choosing whether to support the Syracusans, support the Athenians, or chart the precarious waters of neutrality. Finally, as in the case of the Corcyraean crisis, the war between Athens and Sparta renewed when the Spartans judged that the Athenians had definitively broken the terms of their treaty.[59]

With Athenian forces still engaged from Macedonia to Thrace and across the Aegean, the addition of a new expedition of this size and scope was a major undertaking that would certainly strain Athenian resources and resolve. Nonetheless, the Athenians listened with interest when their delegation and the accompanying Egestaeans reported back. With the delegation came sixty talents of silver, the cost of sixty ships for a month —presumably the sixty ships the Egestaeans were asking for.

While this display of wealth was encouraging, Thucydides hints that the silver may have been part of a deliberate deception staged to give the Athenians further motivation to do what they already intended to do. Thucydides, by now almost ten years into his two decades of exile, was able to draw on information not available to or discounted by the leaders of Athens. Traveling through the Peloponnese and as far north as his family lands in Thrace, he gathered reports from a wide range of sources and from others, like him, not always inclined to suppress conflicting or unpopular opinions.[60] From such sources, he learned that Athens was likely duped. "The report was encouraging," he wrote, "but untrue, particularly on the question of the money which was said to be available in large quantities."[61] Not for the last time, a great power was drawn into a distant foreign expedition on the false promise of substantial financial and physical local support.

Bolstered by this false evidence, with the veneer of honoring ties of culture and alliance commitments, and under the pretense of preventing future threats, the Athenians readied for war in Sicily. There was a great debate in the Assembly over whether to launch an expedition for Sicily.

On one side, opposing the expedition, was the elder statesman Nicias who was wealthy, accomplished, and conservative. Advocating for the expedition was Alcibiade who was brilliant, ambitious, and thoroughly without scruple.

Alcibiades's relationship with his homeland was complex. As the comic poet Aristophanes recorded in his satirical play *The Frogs*, Athens "loves and hates and longs to have him back."[62] Thucydides placed some of the blame for Athens's eventual downfall squarely on the shoulders of Alcibiades. As he recorded: "most people became frightened at a quality in him which was beyond the normal and showed itself both in the lawlessness of his private life and the habits and spirit in which he acted on all occasions."[63] Alcibiades's ambition, shared by other young aristocrats like him, turned Athenian politics away from the noble path Pericles had set. In Thucydides's view, most of these unworthy successors, whether blue bloods of the elite or populist demagogues, were guilty of "striving for first position... [and] were inclined to indulge popular whim even in matters of state policy." Through this shortsightedness, they "brought about their own fall by entangling themselves in internal disputes."[64] And it was a combination of internal disputes and demagoguery-fueled hubris that sent Athens on its fateful expedition against Syracuse.

THE SICILY DEBATE: POLICIES AND PERSONALITIES

Ironically, it was Nicias, the primary author of the Fifty Year's Peace (which often bears his name in subsequent accounts), who was appointed as one of the three *strategoi* for the Sicilian campaign. Disapproving of his assignment, he appeared before the Assembly to argue that going to Sicily was a mistake. Athens had only recently recovered from the plague and a decade and a half of war. The *polis* was still confronting immediate threats on the Greek mainland. The challenges faced by the expedition were greater than Athenians would admit. "[T]his is the wrong time for such adventures," he argued. "[T]he objects of your ambitions are not to be gained easily. In going to Sicily you are leaving many enemies behind you, and you apparently want to make new ones there and have them also on your hands."[65]

Sparta, he noted, had still not formally broken the treaty of peace he had helped to craft. But that should not be taken as a reason to act in Sicily. In fact, Sparta could use this as a cause to consider the treaty broken and to strike while Athens's forces were divided and over extended. "[W]e have not yet come safely into harbor," he argued in a nautical metaphor designed to appeal to the sea-going Athenians. "[T]his is no time for running risks or for grasping for a new empire before we have secured the one we have already." Furthermore, invasion and conquest would not be the only challenge confronting the Athenians in Sicily. Once defeated, the Syracusans and the other states that Athens sought to conquer would have to be governed from far away.[66]

Nicias is contemptuous of Athens's obligation to its allies in Sicily, who he insultingly dismisses as "some barbarians at Egesta."[67] He is more concerned with matters closer to home: the unresolved rebellions within the empire and the potential for the resumption of direct hostilities with Sparta. In his view, Sparta would be likely to take advantage of Athens dividing its forces to campaign in Sicily and would "eagerly join the Greek Sicilians in offensives against us."[68] He also identified a second layer to the Spartan threat. Athens's first and foremost concern, he said, was not the defense of Egesta from the Syracusans but the defense of Athens from "the oligarchical machinations of Sparta."[69] This final point can be seen as a veiled reference to the domestic unrest in Athens, where many were concerned that there was an oligarchic move to seize power and abolish the democracy. Alcibiades, it was feared, was at the forefront of this group.

After Nicias's speech, Alcibiades, the leading proponent of the expedition, came forward to speak. He took the opportunity to strike back at Nicias, who was his political and personal rival. First, he took issue with the personal attack by Nicias against him and the younger generation of Athenians. Their rivalry was actually more than just two individuals at the top of their class of elites who had a personal, visceral dislike for each other. They represented polar opposite generations whose differences reflected political divides in the city that preceded the Sicilian debate and followed on through the post-Sicily downward spiral that ended Athenian democracy.

Alcibiades took the opportunity to praise himself and his achievements and then denigrated the military challenge posed by the armies of Sicily. Athens was capable of simultaneously handling threats both at home and abroad. He spoke of the duty to those who had called for Athens to come to their aid. Finally, he warned that the greater danger was inaction. Waging war would ensure that the city "will constantly be gaining new experiences and growing more used to defend itself not by speeches, but in action."[70]

Nicias countered with a thorough litany of the forces Athens would require for success in the hopes of using the purported cost to deter Athens from the undertaking. The expedition would require at least one hundred ships, not sixty. Ships would have to be diverted from Athens's commercial fleet to serve as transport, with allies adding more ships to the total. More than five-thousand infantry and a force of cavalry from Athens and other cities would need to be organized and sent. The expedition would require considerable supplies and logistics management. If the Assembly did not provide what he enumerated, Nicias was prepared to step aside rather than lead what he perceived to be an inadequate force.[71]

Thucydides concludes that Nicias' intent was to cause the Assembly to pause and soberly reflect on the costs of such an adventure. If so, his plan backfired spectacularly. Nicias' appeal only served to make the challenge more appealing. His reason reinforced the emotions raised by Alcibiades. The scale of expedition Nicias proposed made it more appropriate for the imperialist designs desired by Alcibiades. Thucydides noted that supporters of the expedition became even more enthusiastic after Nicias' second speech. That enthusiasm in turn swayed some who had first agreed with Nicias. The Assembly gave their *strategos* full authority for the resources he had demanded. The expedition, nearly double in size to the one initially envisaged, would go ahead. Alcibiades had won the day. Ironically, after discounting the value of speech over action, it was his superior rhetorical skills and appeal to the pride and vanity of the Assembly that won the argument in combination with Nicias' self-defeating rhetoric.[72]

The debate between Alcibiades and Nicias further reinforces the importance of domestic politics and the role of individuals in the choices made by states. It was Alcibiades's acknowledged skills that shaped the final decision. Alcibiades's own ambition, combined with his dislike of Nicias, motivated his actions. Athens had confidence in success and was willing to pay the costs. Added to this was the bravery and military prowess of Alcibiades. Even those who disliked him acknowledged his skill in battle. Now he would be one of the three *strategoi* with the glory of future victory within his grasp.

But chance—the ever-present and uncontrolled variable—would intervene. Just as the plague took away the leadership and vision of Pericles early in the war, a seemingly random event would alter the fortunes of the force sent to Athens. In the days before the expedition was meant to sail to Sicily, *hermai*—sculptures of male heads and genitals—were defaced throughout the city. As the *hermai* were meant to ward off harm and evil, this was seen as both a serious crime and a feared omen. Witnesses claimed that a group of drunken men had committed this blasphemy. The thorough and coordinated nature of the action demonstrated a degree of organization and forethought that undermines attributing the cause of this act simply to the random vandalism of a group of drunks. The rumor at the time, though not proven, was that Alcibiades was among those taking part.[73] It is equally possible that Alcibiades's rivals engineered the scandal in an attempt to destroy him.

These rivals were quick to declare Alcibiades's guilt. They pointed to his disregard for the conventions of public and private behavior as evidence that he had committed this sacrilege. More damaging still were accusations that questioned his support for Athenian democracy itself. According to this line of attack, the desecrations were not just the random act of a drunken party celebrating their imminent departure for war, but the first steps in a calculated attempt to overthrow the state.[74] Alcibiades, whose popularity was at its height and who stood at the head of a massive military force poised for political and financial gain, pushed for an immediate trial. Better to execute him now, he argued, then to send a force to war with a man under such serious charges in command. In spite of his offer, Alcibiades was refused an immediate trial and instead was allowed to depart at the head of the expedition. His enemies doubtlessly considered it unwise to try him while he had a powerful army at his back. Alcibiades's legitimacy and effectiveness, however, had been diminished despite any clear evidence of his guilt.[75]

Domestic political divisions and internal suspicion now hung over the entire expedition, but the Athenians went forward undeterred. In Syracuse, word arrived of the Athenian preparations. This set off a domestic political debate in Sicily. What was at issue was not whether to confront an invading force. The Syracusans had no intention of following the Melian example. While both sides of the debate in Syracuse agreed that a defense must be mounted, some expressed suspicions that the fear of Athenian attack would be cause for the suspension of democratic rule. The Syracusan statesman Athenagoras argued that there were those in Syracuse who would create and spread rumors of invasion as a means of securing greater political power. Syracuse must be made ready and Syracusan would prevail but not as a means to greater power for a select few. As if to prove his point, debate was cut off and the Assembly dissolved.[76]

LAUNCHING THE TRIREMES

In spite of the cloud hanging over Alcibiades, as the Athenians gathered to see off their expeditionary force, there was great fanfare and high confidence. Each of the captains "went to extreme lengths to prove his own ship the best in both splendor and speed."[77] The assembled ships and troops were more than just a display of military might. Thucydides notes that the investment of public funds, as well as private money, was vast. After the ceremonies and speeches and prayers, the soldiers and sailors drank from cups of gold and silver. Once the ships launched, the ships' captains, full of cheerful confidence, raced each other from the Piraeus harbor to the island of Aegina.[78] It was a splendid sight to behold —an armada such as the Greek world had never seen set on a mission of unmatched ambition:

> [W]hat made this armament the talk of Greece was the astonishing spectacle, let alone the overwhelming scale of military force brought against its objective: and it was recognized that this was the longest expeditionary voyage ever undertaken from a home state, and an enterprise of unprecedented ambition in the relation of intended gain to present holding.[79]

The Athenian fleet then met its allied contingents at Corcyra. Together, they comprised a naval force of one hundred and thirty-six ships (a quarter of these from allies) divided into three squadrons, each commanded by a *strategos*. The infantry hoplites numbered five thousand one hundred, two thousand two hundred of whom were Athenian, and there were more than one thousand three hundred archers, cavalry, and other troops from Athens and five other states. Cargo ships carried food, tools, siege equipment, skilled craftsman, bakers, and laborers. Trailing the fleet were merchant ships hoping to engage in trade.[80]

When the armada arrived in Sicily, Nicias and Alcibiades disagreed over how to proceed. Nicias preferred to sail to the western tip of the island to intimidate Selinunte and confirm the support of Egesta, making a show of force along the way. His primary preoccupation was to ensure that the Egestaeans would provide the forces and resources as promised. If these resources were not forthcoming, he argued, the Athenians should return home. Alcibiades would have none of this. He recommended fomenting rebellion against Syracuse on the eastern coast of the island, while Lamachus, the third *strategos* sharing command of the expedition, called for an immediate attack on Syracuse itself.[81]

As the discussions continued, the Athenians searched for a place to make their initial base. Expecting to be greeted by allies, the Athenians, instead, were unable to find places that would allow them to land and establish their presence. Those who believed that Athenian troops would be welcomed and supported by various actors in Sicily who appreciated Athens's intervention were facing the first of many disappointments.[82]

Before full operations could be launched in Sicily, the Athenians suffered a significant setback, not on the battlefield but because of domestic politics. The uproar over the defacing of the statues of the gods continued to grow. Accusations were being made. Rumors were given the weight of truth. Alcibiades had first been allowed to sail with the fleet. Now, the Athenian Assembly sent the state galley *Salaminia* demanding his recall to Athens to stand trial. If found guilty, he would be executed. Alcibiades set out to return to Athens. When his ship put in at the small city of Thurii in the instep of the Italian boot, he slipped away. Alcibiades—who had argued for this expansion of the war, who had spoken of patriotism to the Athenian Assembly, who led the fleet to Sicily and knew all its plans, its strengths, and its weaknesses—would next be seen in Sparta, providing advice on how best to defeat Athens.[83] Domestic politics drove the decision to remove Alcibiades from command and, as a result, weakened the available Athenian generalship in Sicily. These developments, however, are distinct from the sort of domestic protests and attempts to undermine support for a foreign expedition that defined the later American experience in Vietnam, in spite of modern attempts to create an analogy between the two.[84] Athenian support for the campaign in Sicily was not undermined by the fall of Alcibiades; they simply wanted other leaders in place to see it through.

The fall of Alcibiades meant that Nicias was now the primary *strategos* in command. The fight with Syracuse began in earnest, with Athens winning early victories. But for Syracuse and its numerous allies the longer strategic odds were in their favor. The defending alliance grew in strength and confidence. More allies, both in Sicily and on the mainland, joined with Syracuse. As predicted by Nicias, the continuing demands of warfare throughout Hellas began to take its toll on Athens. Sparta, with the urging and advice of Alcibiades, encouraged those willing to attack Athens at home or to sail to Syracuse to join the fight there.

Still, the Peace of Nicias held; Sparta refused to resume hostilities against Athens. Then Athens, seeing their battlefield successes in Sicily reversed by forces linked with Sparta and responding to pressure from allies, sent thirty ships to raid the coast of the Spartan homeland. Compared to battles waged before and after, the physical costs to Sparta were small. However, the political value to Sparta was enormous. It could now publicly declare that it was not the one violating its sacred oath. The treaty was broken. Sparta and Athens were now directly at war again.[85]

Beyond a small token force, Sparta did not send troops and ships against the Athenians in Sicily. It did not have to. Corinth was the Spartan ally with the one asset that Sparta lacked and which Syracuse needed—a large and capable navy. Corinthian hatred of Athens was undimmed. In Syracuse, Corinth saw an opportunity to deal Athenian power a major blow and intended to make its chance count. Corinth's naval prowess predated and informed that of Athens. Now, Corinth led a growing fleet with ships from other, smaller *poleis*. These states had suffered what they must under Athenian hegemony; now they were decisively doing what they willed. Joining them was a Syracusan fleet growing in skill and confidence.[86]

Athenian victories became fewer and more costly. Though Nicias knew the situation was growing desperate, he tried to rally the troops of Athens and their allies. Defeatism and despair began to rise in the Athenian ranks. Confronted with a deteriorating situation, Nicias sent a message to Athens asking for more ships and troops and urging a change in strategy. Rather than relying on the tradition of entrusting verbal communiqués to messengers, Nicias composed a letter to be delivered and read in the Assembly. He did not hold back his candor or his anger. "[W]e, who thought we were the besiegers, have become in fact the besieged."[87] Athenian commanders, who had once drunk from golden cups, who had raced each other for fun at the expedition's inception, now had ships whose "timbers have rotted" and had crews who were "not what they were." Nicias lamented further that

> the enemy has as many or more ships than we have, and keeps us in constant expectation of having to face an attack... the slightest falling-off on the efficiency of the watch we keep would mean the loss of our supplies, which even now are difficult enough to bring in.

Allied troops were falling off, slaves were deserting, and enemy cavalry was producing frequent casualties.[88] "But the greatest of all my troubles," he informed the people of Athens

> is that since you are by nature so difficult to control, I, the general, am unable to put a stop to all this. I know the Athenian character from experience: you like to be told pleasant news, but if things do not turn out in the way you have been led to expect, then you blame your informants.[89]

Nicias's force needed help immediately and the Athenians responded with more ships, more troops, and more funds. New *strategoi* were sent to share the demands and responsibilities of command with Nicias.[90]

The Athenians were not the only ones receiving messages from the front lines. Corinth, in particular, was growing in confidence.[91] The Spartans, now freed from the constraints of their treaty, prepared to invade Attica. "But what chiefly encouraged the Spartans to act with energy was their belief that Athens, with two wars on her hands—one against them and one against the Sicilians—would now be easier to crush."[92]

In spite of the difficulties, Athenian troops continued to fight. There were victories against the Syracusan navy, but supply convoys were still regularly intercepted. The relief force was being delayed and reduced. Allies were not arriving in time or in large enough numbers. A force from Thrace was sent home when it arrived too late to join its assigned convoy and was deemed too expensive to be kept on hand for the next opportunity to travel to Sicily. Athens was suffering great economic losses from Spartan attacks.[93] Nicias informed his weary troops, "[Y]ou have no more ships like these left in your dockyards, and no reserve of men fit to fight."[94]

Athenian troops then suffered a series of decisive defeats in close succession with the final series of engagements fought as the Athenians and their allies retreated inland, fighting as they went. At the river Assinarus, their exhausted, starving, and greatly reduced ranks broke. The Peloponnesians and Syracusans slaughtered their enemies as they desperately tried to drink from the river. Nicias finally surrendered. The surviving prisoners were herded into an open stone quarry, where they began to die from wounds, exposure, starvation, thirst, and disease. The Spartan commander, Gylippus, had planned to bring Nicias to Sparta as a gift to his patrons and allies but others (particularly the Corinthians, Thucydides writes) did not want him spared.[95] "He was killed, a man who of all the Hellenes in his time, least deserved to come to so miserable an end, since the whole of his life had been devoted to the study and the practice of virtue."[96]

IN THE WAKE OF SICILY

"When the news reached Athens, for a long-time people would not believe it, even though they were given precise information from the very soldiers who had been present at the event and had escaped."[97] As Nicias had said in his letter from Sicily, the Athenians did not handle bad news well. Thucydides, ever critical of what he considered the constant and fickle U-turns that characterized democratic politics, recorded that the Athenians "turned against the public speakers who had been in favor of the expedition, as though they themselves had not voted for it, and also became angry with the prophets and soothsayers."[98]

Beyond the political blame game, the Athenians were also confronting the harsh realities of empty coffers and inadequate forces. Panic spread at the fear that the victorious Peloponnesians would turn from their victory in Sicily and focus on Athens and its lands. Defections began from the Delian League, further undermining Athenian power. But the Athenians would not simply give in. They frantically began to build ships and seek funds. In a statement of incisive cynicism, Thucydides did give some begrudging credit to the democracy, recording that "like all democracies, now that they were terrified, they were ready to put everything in order."[99]

Athens was vulnerable in the extreme. Because it had done what it willed, it was now forced to suffer what it must. Thucydides's account of the war continues on for another two years after the disaster in Sicily, ending in mid-sentence while recounting events in 411. He chronicled the fall of Athenian democracy to the rule of the Four Hundred, which represented the interests of leading oligarchs. One of their first acts was to communicate with King Agis II of Sparta, "saying that they were willing to make peace and expected him to be readier to agree terms with them than with the fickle democracy they had supplanted."[100] Sensing Athenian division and weakness, however, Agis refused their offer.

The Athenian elite had had enough of the war. The imperial economy that had prospered and enriched them with tribute, trade, duties, and agricultural bounty had been practically destroyed by the decades of conflict. The elite had borne a heavy financial burden. The long war had dramatically reduced the number of those fit to serve in the military (by as much as two-thirds) and the capability of that shrinking number of citizens to pay taxes and make contributions to the war effort—voluntary or otherwise. Athenian elites paid an enormous share of the state's costs. They "produced tragic and comic dramas; paid for choral competitions, dancers, athletic contests, and trireme races," they even equipped triremes for war at their own expense.[101] Paying the greatest share of expenses, the oligarchs moved to seize the political control that they thought was theirs by right. In doing so, however, they ignored their own role in the Athenian catastrophe. Even Thucydides, who was not an admirer of radical democracy, was critical of the actions of many of the oligarchs. He believed that the pursuit of "private ambition and private profit led to policies which were bad both for the Athenians themselves and for their allies."[102] That the Athenians were tired of war in 411 is also evident in the literary record. The most famous extant play from that year is the comedy *Lysistrata*, by Aristophanes. Irreverent as ever, Aristophanes's play centers on an invented plot by the women of Greece to band together and end the war by denying sex to their partners, bawdily employing all manner of sexual jokes to mock the endless war devouring the people of Athens and Sparta, alike.

Neither Aristophanes's play nor the political upheavals in Athens brought an end to the war. The contest between the radical democrats and oligarchs was at the heart of the internal divisions plaguing Athens. Nicias had alluded to them before the expedition to Sicily. Now, they were in full view. Following the oligarchic coup, a large Athenian force on the island of Samos mutinied against the Four Hundred, which also faced opposition within the city from "moderate" oligarchs[103] and democrats. Soon, the Four Hundred were deposed by a popular assembly and replaced by a government of "the Five Thousand (to be constituted of all those who could provide their own hoplite armor)." A new constitution, which overturned key elements of the Periclean democracy, was instituted.[104] Thucydides approved of the new political order:

> [N]ow for the first time, at least in my lifetime, the Athenians enjoyed a political system of substantial and obvious merit, which blended the interest of the few and the many without extremes, and began to restore the city from the wretched situation into which it had fallen. The Five Thousand also voted for the recall of Alcibiades and other exiles with him.[105]

Thucydides may have objectively agreed with the tenets of the new
ordering of Athenian society, but it is also likely that he owed the new
regime a personal debt as one of the political exiled probably recalled to
Athens during this time. Alcibiades, whose exile was also ended, again
assumed command. He, and the new oligarchic constitution, would not
last long. Soon, Alcibiades was forced to flee Athens once more and
a democratic regime was restored. It was this democracy that finally
surrendered to Sparta in 404.

Sparta's victory put an end to Athenian democracy and the city's
"Golden Age." A brief rule of "Thirty Tyrants" supported by Sparta was
instituted. Within a year, they, too, were gone, and the democracy was
restored once more. Although Athens reclaimed its democracy, it would
never reclaim its former glories. The new democracy held few of the
ideals enunciated by Pericles and produced even fewer of its glories.
Work on the monuments of the Acropolis was halted. Athena, no longer
a bringer of victory, left Athens little tribute to enshrine her praise in
marble. The great tragedians were dead, never to be succeeded. The
comedian Aristophanes survived and wrote plays after the end of the
war, still happy to lampoon the political elite. Plato proved a worthy
successor to Socrates, but his old master was condemned to death and
drank hemlock for the "corruption of youth."

Across the Hellenic world, the long, costly war had taken an irreparable
toll on the lives of citizens, public treasuries, and the credibility and
legitimacy of government. Even Sparta would soon fall from its position
of newfound dominance. Persia even tried to reassert itself. But it was
others who, each in turn, ultimately took control of the once powerful
city-states of Greece. By 336, the Macedonians had defeated the Athenians
and the Thebans to establish firm control of the Hellenic states. Then
came the Romans, who admired and adopted much of Greek culture
but also razed cities like Corinth and rebuilt them in a Roman image of
what they wished Ancient Greece to be. Then came the Germanic tribes
who sacked Athens, Corinth, Argos, and Sparta. Then came Byzantium,

followed by the Arabs, followed by the Crusaders, the Venetians, and finally the Ottomans, in whose empire the once great Greek states became a backwater. The philosophy and political institutions—or at least their Renaissance approximation—would enjoy a revival in the Italian city-states eighteen centuries after the defeat of Athens. It would be almost two thousand two hundred years before an independent Greece was established.

NOTES

1. Thuc. 1.21 (W).
2. Clifton Truman Daniel, "Adventures With Grandpa Truman" *National Archives* 41, no. 1 (Spring 2009), https://www.archives.gov/publications/prologue/2009/spring/grandpa-truman.html.
3. Thuc. 5.89 (C).
4. Thuc. 1.110.
5. The non-scholarly accounts of these events—and even the synopses and snippets incorporated in scholarly works—are often brief and incomplete. At times, they can be contradictory. For example, the Wikipedia account (which is often both the first and last source consulted by many students) provides a standard summary, which asserts that Athens offered no moral justification for its attack; Athens was motivated solely by its own gain. However, scrolling down well into the online entry reveals three citations supporting the assertion that Melos has provided financial support for Sparta's war effort (en.m.wikipedia.org, *The Siege of Melos,* accessed 14 June 2016).
6. Ober, *Political Dissent in Democratic Athens,* 105.
7. Thauer, *Thucydides and Political Order,* 47.
8. Wasserman, "The Melian Dialogue," 21.
9. Garst, "Thucydides and Neorealism," 3.
10. Clark, "Realism Ancient and Modern," 492.
11. Ibid.
12. Garst, "Thucydides and Neorealism," 17.
13. Doyle, "Thucydidean Realism," 224.
14. Ibid., 228.
15. Bagby, "The Use and Abuse of Thucydides in International Relations," 147.
16. Lebow, "International Relations and Thucydides," 209.
17. Doyle, "Thucydidean Realism," 228.
18. Bagby, "The Use and Abuse of Thucydides in International Relations," 147.
19. Ibid., 144. See the discussion of this episode in chapter 6.
20. Thuc. 3.91.
21. Thuc. 5.84 (H).
22. de Ste. Croix, "The Character of the Athenian Empire," 13.

23. The Peace of Nicias (421), analyzed in chapter 4.
24. Thauer, *Thucydides and Political Order*, 47.
25. Measuring 58 square miles, Melos is the twenty-third largest of Greece's 1,500 islands. Today, it supports a population of 5,000 inhabitants.
26. Fornara, *Archaic Times to the End of the Peloponnesian War*, 59.
27. Thuc. 5.85 (W).
28. See the discussion of this event in chapter 3.
29. Thuc. 5.86 (H).
30. Thuc. 5.89 (W).
31. Thuc. 5.14-25; Kagan, *The Peloponnesian War*, 191-209; Bagnall, *The Peloponnesian War*, 183-200.
32. Fornara, Archaic Times to the End of the Peloponnesian War, 83.
33. Ibid., 84.
34. Assessments of value in ancient economies are always challenging. As further context, we know, for example that the 16 slaves in the house of Alcibiades (in 414) were assessed at values between 72 and 301 drachmas each.
35. Thuc. 7.28.
36. Ibid., 5.84.
37. Garst, "Thucydides and Neorealism," 14.
38. Thuc. 5.114.
39. Thuc. 5.103 (W).
40. Ibid., 5.115.
41. Unfortunately, there is too little evidence to speculate whether this was, by coincidence, the commander's actual name or whether Thucydides intended it as a satirical quip against Athenian policy over Melos.
42. Thuc. V.116 (H).
43. Thuc. 3.47.
44. Garst, "Thucydides and Neorealism," 13.
45. Thuc. 3.50.
46. Bagby, "The Use and Abuse of Thucydides in International Relations," 146.
47. Euripides, *The Trojan Women*, 93–96.
48. Thuc. 5.116-6.1 (W).
49. De Romilly, *The Mind of Thucydides*, 24.
50. Thuc. 6.1–6.
51. Thuc. 6.1 (W).
52. Thuc. 3.86 (H).
53. Sometimes also written as "Segesta."

54. Fornara, *Archaic Times to the End of the Peloponnesian War*, 81.
55. Thuc. 6.6.
56. Fornara, *Archaic Times to the End of the Peloponnesian War*, 125.
57. Thuc. 5.4.
58. Thuc. 6.6 (W).
59. Thuc. 1.88, 6.105.
60. Kagan, *Thucydides*, 196.
61. Thuc. 6.7 (W).
62. Aristophanes, *Frogs*, 1425.
63. Thuc. 6.15 (W).
64. Thuc. 2.65 (H).
65. Thuc. 6.9-10 (W).
66. Ibid., 6.10.
67. Thuc. 6.11 (H).
68. Ibid., VI.10.
69. Thuc. 6.11 (W).
70. Ibid., 6.15-19.
71. Thuc. 6.21–23.
72. Ibid., 6.24–46.
73. Ibid., 6.27.
74. Ibid., 6.28.
75. Ibid., 6.27–29.
76. Ibid., 6.35–41.
77. Thuc. 6.31 (H).
78. Thuc. 6.32.
79. Thuc. 6.31 (H).
80. Thuc. 6.42–44.
81. Ibid., 6.47–49.
82. Ibid., 6.50–52.
83. Ibid., 6.60–61, 88–93.
84. Turner, "Address to Chicago Council Navy League of the United States Lake Shore Club."
85. Thuc. 6.105; 7.18.
86. Ibid., 8.1–7.
87. Thuc. 7.10–11 (W).
88. Ibid., 7.12–13.
89. Thuc. 7.15 (W).
90. Thuc. 7.16–17.
91. Ibid., 7.17.

92. Thuc. 7.18 (W).
93. Thuc. 7.27–29.
94. Thuc. 7.64. (W).
95. Thuc. 7.72–87.
96. Thuc. 7.86 (W).
97. Ibid., 8.1.
98. Ibid.
99. Ibid.
100. Thuc. 8.70.
101. Kagan, *The Fall of the Athenian Empire*, 111.
102. Thuc. 2.65 (W).
103. "Moderate" in the sense that they favored a broader base for political decision-making than the Four Hundred.
104. Thuc. 8.97 (W).
105. Ibid.

CHAPTER 6

"FOR ALL TIME?"

ENDURING DYNAMICS OF GREAT POWER COMPETITION

"It will be enough for me, however, if these words of mine are judged useful by those who want to understand clearly the events which happened in the past and which (human nature being what it is) will, at some time or other and in much the same ways, be repeated in the future."[1]

—Thucydides

"I doubt seriously whether a man can think with full wisdom and deep convictions regarding certain of the basic international issues today who has not at least reviewed in his mind the period of the Peloponnesian War and the Fall of Athens." [2]

—Secretary of State George Marshall, February 22, 1947

Thucydides's exploration of great power politics was innovative when it was posited in the fifth century BCE. Interpreting geopolitics through the actions of great powers has since—in no small part due to his contribution—become fundamental to the discipline of international relations. Xenophon, Thucydides's immediate successor, continued the history of the twists and turns of Greek politics through the eclipse of Spartan power down through the first half of the fourth century, with a focus on great power politics. Polybius, another Greek, wrote his

famous work to explain the rise of Rome, chronicling its victories over
the Carthaginians, the Macedonians, and the various Greek leagues that
dominated politics in the third and second centuries. How Rome rose to
be the dominant power in the Mediterranean, defeating Carthaginian and
Greek rivals, was the focus of his work. In this emphasis, as in much else,
both Xenophon and Polybius reflected a clear Thucydidean influence.

In *The History*, Thucydides posits that great powers make momentous
decisions for significant reasons. While identifying the relevance of
systemic level factors, he also provides us a useful lens to understand
what happens in geopolitics through perception, debate, and choices.
He emphasizes the importance of domestic politics and the agency of
individual actors. Whereas shortcuts and shorthands give us an often
unsatisfactory two-dimensional image, a comprehensive reading of *The
History* tells us even more about the dynamics of great power competition
in the modern world.

The historical evidence for the period beyond the (premature) conclusion of Thucydides's work confirms the broader lessons imbedded in his
work about great power politics: the fundamental flexibility of alliances,
the focus of policymakers on achieving balance, and the endurance of
great power competition—even after the conclusion of "hegemonic wars,"
which are supposed to bring such things to an end. Even when using
evidence from Thucydides to build theory on such core issues as great
power competition, scholars treat his work carelessly. Many IR scholars
use the war Thucydides describes to support the view that hegemonic
wars are "followed by long periods of peace built upon a fundamental
reordering of the system by the victor(s)."[3] In their view, hegemonic wars
are underpinned by "the idea that the basis of power and social order is
undergoing a fundamental transformation."[4] Thucydides's case, however
—particularly the events beyond the conclusion of *The History* and then
the subsequent history of the Hellenic world—contradicts these simplistic
observations. Instead, we see great power competition dominated by the
concern for balance and the durability of conflict even after the conclusion

of "hegemonic" wars as other powers continue to compete for security and position. This chapter will explore these themes using the history of events after Thucydides, particularly the conclusion of the Peloponnesian War and the series of bloody conflicts that followed in its wake.

Securing Peace: A Story of Balance

Balance is a fundamental element in Thucydides's *The History*. Conflict was the option when balance failed. Resistance or realignment was the choice when the existing distribution of power seemed unfavorable. The search for order could even be the determining factor in choosing policy towards a defeated foe. This was never more significant than in Sparta's policy at the conclusion of the war in 404. The question confronting Spartan policymakers was the fate of Athens. As described earlier, Athens was the most populous, richest, most powerful, and most culturally significant individual *polis* within the Hellenic world. As a result, its fate represented a particular challenge to the Spartans.

Sparta's allies had few doubts about what should be done. At the assembly of the Peloponnesian League—called to debate the fate of Athens—the Theban Erianthus suggested that the city should be razed to the ground, its temples pulled down, and its land left as pasture for sheep.[5] Corinthian representatives, not surprisingly, concurred with this draconian proposal. The vehemence of its two most powerful allies on this issue appears to have given Spartan policymakers pause. Meting out such comprehensive violence was not unheard of, but to impose such a policy on the Athenians was an extraordinary suggestion. In 427, the Spartans had followed through on the Theban request to destroy the *polis* of Plataea.[6] At the time, the Plataeans made their appeal for mercy through the lens of history. It is, they argued, a

> terrible thing that Sparta should destroy Plataea, and that the city whose name your fathers inscribed on the tripod at Delphi for its honors in the battle [where the Persians were defeated by a

unified Greek force in 479 BCE] should be by you, and for the sake of Thebes, wiped off the map of Hellas.[7]

Their appeal fell on deaf Spartan ears. The entire adult male population was executed. As Thucydides tersely observed, "[i]t was largely, or entirely, because of Thebes that the Spartans acted so mercilessly towards the Plataeans; they considered that at this stage of the war the Thebans were useful to them. This was the end of Plataea."[8]

Two decades later, however, the Spartans hesitated to follow through with such a radical proposal. What had changed? An analysis of this decision is rarely part of debates about Thucydides because his history does not include these events. Perhaps because it does not appear in Thucydides's account, Sparta's decision occupies surprisingly little space in both the subsequent primary and secondary historical source record. Xenophon, whose *Hellenica* chronicles the period between 411 and 362, explains the conflicting options and outcome in a single paragraph.[9] Plutarch, the biographer, writing in the second century CE, devotes a similarly brief space to the subject in his life of Lysander—the Spartan commander responsible for the final siege of Athens.[10] The geographer Pausanias, writing a half century later than Plutarch, mentions only the initial suggestion by Sparta's allies that Athens be destroyed "root and branch."[11] He does not address any subsequent debate that took place to convince the Spartans to reject this option and show restraint instead.

There is almost no account in the ancient sources for the debate that followed the allied proposal to destroy Athens. This suggests that ancient historians were not surprised by Sparta's decision because, based on the evidence we have, they felt little need to explain it. To their minds, it was logical that Sparta would not eliminate Athens. As we have seen in the case of Plataea and Melos, it was possible to kill off small states. But, even in the ancient world, war rarely eliminated major powers from the scene. This outcome was the result of a combination of intent and capability. Ancient states lacked the intent and, very often, the capacity to kill off great power rivals. In the ancient world, "[i]t was rarely possible... for one

side to destroy its enemy utterly in war, unless the states involved were
very small and one had an overwhelming advantage."[12] Sparta's decision
may have been par for the course, but it still requires an explanation,
particularly since the utter destruction of Athens was what Sparta's
allies urged.

Among modern historians, neither Hanson nor Bagnall consider the
question of why Sparta did not destroy Athens.[13] Kagan touches on
the decision across a few pages at the end of *The Peloponnesian War*.[14]
He attributes Sparta's decision to show mercy to their concerns about
the potential power vacuum that would be created in northern Greece
if Athens were destroyed. Kagan argues that Thebes, Sparta's ally,
could have used its increased power after the destruction of Athens to
challenge Spartan hegemony. Kagan's argument has the ring of truth,
but it is cursory. Since he is writing a narrative history, interspersed with
analytical elements, this question is only of passing interest and is not
linked to any theoretical implications.

Tritle comes to a similar conclusion in an even more abbreviated space.
His argument is more supposition than certainty, inflected with a dose
of conditionality. The Spartans "may have recognized that allies like
Corinth and Thebes might pose a threat... and might have imagined future
difficulties with them now."[15] Overall, in the secondary sources, we see
little discussion of a Spartan policy of exterminating Athens, and only a
cursory explanation for why such a policy would have been a poor choice.

It is a shame Thucydides died before he could write about the conclusion
of the war. Perhaps his account would offer a "truest cause" for Sparta's
decision. As it stands, the historical record as presented in Xenophon and
other ancient writers offers slightly different explanations. Xenophon
attributes Spartan mercy to gratitude and memory. He writes that the
Spartans felt that they could not "enslave a Greek city which had done
great service amid the greatest perils that had befallen Greece [the Persian
Wars]."[16] This was history. A similar appeal to history, as we observed
above, had failed to save the Plataeans. In the present, the implication

was the Sparta's leaders needed Athens (at least its potential as a naval power) to protect the Greek city-states from renewed Persian intervention or even another Persian invasion. This may have been persuasive, but Athens's primary power—particularly to oppose Persia—was maritime, and the peace treaty Sparta imposed reduced Athens's navy to nothing more than a token force.

Pausanias recoiled at the suggestion that Athens be destroyed since it would violate the terms of a Spartan oath.[17] Given how religious and punctilious the Spartans generally were, this argument has merit. Oaths were certainly important to the Spartans, and religious obligations were likely to have played prominently in their thinking, although it is unlikely that, by itself, such a factor would have proven decisive. For example, it was only after the failure to achieve an easy victory at the start of the war, after the defeat at Sphacteria, and after the conclusion of the Peace of Nicias that the Spartans considered that in declaring war in 432, they were violating a sacred oath. This guilt was entirely retrospective, based on failure in the present. Enjoying success in 404, earlier oaths would probably not have prevented the Spartans from exercising vengeance if they considered it to be in their interests.

Plutarch's argument, as presented in his biography of Lysander, is also one grounded in morality. In his account, a Spartan ally from the city of Phocis recited a verse of Euripides, and "all [the Spartans] were moved to compassion, and felt it to be a cruel deed to abolish and destroy a city which was so famous and produced such poets."[18] There is, perhaps, some irony to this explanation because the Spartans were often the subject of mockery (not least from the Athenians) for being unlettered, "laconic," and unartistic. They certainly did not prioritize poetry, plays, and the arts in the manner that the Athenians did although it is probably an exaggeration to argue that they were largely illiterate.[19] It is possible that Athenian culture was an argument against the annihilation of Athens, but it is also not, by itself, entirely convincing.

Beyond these reasons, a source from the second century CE, the Macedonian author Polyaenus, offers an explanation based on the values of *realpolitik*. Writing in a volume on strategy (dedicated to the Roman emperors Marcus Aurelius and Lucius Verus), he records that:

> When the Lacedaemonians and their allies were debating whether they should entirely destroy the city of Athens, Lysander urged many arguments against doing so. He particularly emphasized that Thebes, which was a neighboring state, would thereby be rendered more powerful, and a more formidable enemy to Sparta. Whereas, if they could preserve the loyalty of Athens, under the government of tyrants, they might watch over the actions of the Thebans from nearby, and keep them from growing too great. Lysander's advice was approved, and they were prevailed upon to give up the plan of destroying Athens.[20]

Polyaenus' explanation certainly has the ring of truth. It accurately predicted that a Spartan ally, Thebes, was in fact a threat to its newly won hegemony within the Hellenic world. Although Polyaenus had the benefit of hindsight—knowing that Theban power would eventually overthrow Sparta—there was already evidence, both in Thucydides and in Xenophon, that Thebes was becoming more and more difficult for Sparta to control. Athens, made cooperative under the rule of a narrow oligarchy (the Thirty Tyrants), which owed their position to Sparta, could play the role of balancer.

The cursory nature of each of these explanations from ancient and modern sources leaves us with little empirical evidence to discount them but also little to depend on from a theoretical perspective. The war had seen many norms of behavior ignored or overturned. It is possible that Sparta turned from destroying Athens because it valued its poetry or because of some moral qualms, but the more convincing argument is that Sparta felt its political interests, based on a balance of power calculation, were best served by preserving Athens. An independent Athens provided a buffer against Theban territorial ambitions across central Greece. This theory is also supportable based on an investigation of the broader historical record before the Peloponnesian War. Using Athens to balance against Thebes was a consistent trend in Sparta foreign policy, going back at least half a century.[21] Athenian power could also serve as a potential counterweight against the influence of Corinth, particularly in terms of economic and naval power. In spite of its diminished navy, Athens also retained the potential to serve the broader Hellenic world in a future conflict with Persia. For these reasons, it seems likely that Sparta did not kill Athens.

Taking the substantive messages Thucydides repeats throughout his work concerning the importance of the balance of power and the fluidity of alliances, the Spartans recognized that today's enemy can be tomorrow's friend and that today's friend can become tomorrow's rival as the balance of power shifts. For this reason, they exercised restraint in their dealings with Athens. Sparta offered peace to Athens on the following terms: the Athenians would dismantle their Long Walls, the fortifications linking the city of Athens to the port of Piraeus, they would tear down the fortifications of the Piraeus, they would hand over to the Spartans all but twelve of their ships, and they would allow their exiles (almost certainly pro-Spartan oligarchs) to return to the city. The newly restored democracy would be replaced by a narrow oligarchy (called the Thirty Tyrants), elected at the request of the victorious Spartan commander, Lysander, and supported by a Spartan garrison.

Most significantly, the Athenians would have to be "willing to follow the Spartans as their leaders on land or sea, on whatever campaign the Spartans should order."[22] The phrasing of this agreement, if Xenophon is quoting it precisely, suggests that Sparta was essentially bringing Athens into the Peloponnesian League. The Athenian leaders agreed to the terms. The exiles returned to the city and the Spartans, and their allies, "[w]ith great zeal... dismantled the walls, to the accompaniment of music provided by flute girls, and they believed that that day would be the beginning of freedom for all of Greece."[23] They were sadly mistaken.

Although Thucydides probably did not live long after the defeat of Athens in 404, the dynamics of the events that followed his city's defeat would, nevertheless, have been familiar to him. Realignment and conflict did not stop with the fall of Athens, nor did domestic political disorder. The rule of the "Thirty Tyrants" was brief and bloody. One leading member, Theramenes, who had been instrumental in clinching the final peace treaty with Sparta, was among those purged. A pupil of Socrates, Critias, won infamy for his brutality as the leader of the Thirty, while the philosopher became a critic of the regime. After only eight months, Athenian democrats overthrew the tyrants and reestablished democracy. The Spartans were too disorganized dealing with their own political disruptions to mount any successful interference.

Peace and War

Great power competition remained even after the end of the conflict Thucydides called "the greatest disturbance in the history of the Hellenes."[24] It continued with familiar themes but with surprising results. A brief synopsis of the half century after the end of the Peloponnesian War confirms this observation and contradicts the view, often interpreted from Thucydides, that hegemonic wars stabilize international systems in their wake.

After victory in 404, Sparta continued its involvement in the politics of Asia Minor. Greek mercenaries under Spartan command fought in a Persian civil war. They won the major battle of this conflict (at Cunaxa in 401), but the claimant they supported for the throne was killed. Further Spartan involvement in Asia Minor led one Persian satrap (provincial governor) to approach leaders in Thebes, Corinth, Argos, and Athens with money "to make war against the Spartans."[25] The men of Thebes, Corinth, and Argos accepted the money. Athens demurred. Soon, however, a general war, called the Corinthian War, was set in motion with Sparta and its Peloponnesian allies confronting a coalition of Thebes, Corinth, Athens, and Argos, backed by Persian gold.

In spite of the odds, Sparta acquitted itself well. Victories on land at Nemea (395) and Coronea (394) confirmed Spartan dominance in hoplite battle. Sparta's fleet was defeated at sea at the Battle of Cnidus (394) by a largely Persian fleet under the command of an Athenian admiral, Conon, who had been active in the final stages of the Peloponnesian War. This was an important reversal and closed the brief period of Spartan naval dominance enjoyed since Aegospotami. A deadlock—reminiscent of the early years of the Peloponnesian War—ensued, until the war was brought to a close with the Peace of Antalcidas (387).

Even this agreement—called the King's Peace in antiquity because of the role of the Persian King Artaxerxes II in negotiating it—was insufficient to end the fractious politics of the Hellenic world. By 378, Sparta and Thebes were once more at war. A Spartan army marched north to confront the Thebans. This time, however, Sparta was defeated; its army was routed at the battle of Leuktra in 371. Flush with victory, the Thebans and their allies invaded the Peloponnese, aiming to crush Sparta. They met on the familiar field of Mantinea in 362. Here, Spartan power was definitively shattered. Although the Thebans won the battle, their military and political leaders were killed, and they were unable to follow up their success. The result of the battle was deeply unsatisfying. As Xenophon records with the final sentences of his history:

> When the battle was over, the result was the opposite of what everyone had expected. Given that nearly all of Greece was gathered there and had stood with one side or the other, everyone thought that if a battle occurred, the victor would rule over the defeated and the defeated would be subject to the victor. But the gods so arranged it that each side set up a trophy as if victorious, and both received back their dead under truce as if defeated. And although each side claimed the victory, neither side was seen to have gained anything—no city, territory or increased rule—that they did not have prior to the battle. In Greece, as a whole, there was more uncertainty and disturbance after the battle than there

had been before. To this point, then, let it be written by me. Perhaps someone else will be concerned with that happened after this.[26]

The inconclusive nature of this second battle of Mantinea, however, was temporary. In fact, it precipitated a disaster Sparta had fought to avert for hundreds of years—the collapse of its domestic political order. In the wake of Mantinea, large segments of the *perioikoi* communities rose against the *homoioi*. The helots, supported by Theban forces, launched a full-scale uprising, reestablishing their independence in the newly reconstituted *polis* of Messenia. Devoid of their clients and partners, the Spartan *homoioi* were simply not numerous enough to mount a successful resistance. Spartan power would never recover.

More than a century of practically unremitting conflict among the Hellenic states had left them exhausted. No *polis* had achieved a universal hegemony. Athens, Sparta, and Thebes had all bid for dominance and failed. Ares, the God of War, who Homer described as "that baleful scourge of mortal men," had more than lived up to his epithet.[27] In the years that followed the second battle of Mantinea, Thebes allied with Athens to oppose the rise of the Macedonians under the leadership of Philip II. His son Alexander III, better known as Alexander the Great, would eventually put the entire Hellenic world under his control, before the premature fracturing of his empire and the coming of Rome. Those stories, however, are far beyond the scope of the present work. Here, it suffices to observe that the period between 411 and 362 (covered by Xenophon) confirmed the flexibility in diplomatic alignment that characterized the world of Thucydides. This endured after his death and continued to define the politics of the Hellenic world until its end. It is a future Thucydides anticipated, one characterized by the enduring struggle for balance, not the peace many modern scholars attribute to the conclusion of a hegemonic war.

NOTES

1. Ibid., 1.22.
2. Conner, *Thucydides*, 3.
3. Schweller and Wohlforth, "Power Test," 78.
4. Gilpin, "The Theory of Hegemonic War," 602.
5. Plutarch, *Lysander*, 15.2.
6. Existing on the border between Attica and Boeotia, the *polis* of Plataea was a battleground for Athens and Thebes. The Plataean alliance with Athens began in 519. As Thucydides describes, Thebes' secret attack on Plataea began the war.
7. Thuc. 3.57.
8. Ibid., 3.68.
9. Xenophon, *Hellenica*, 2.2.19–20.
10. Plutarch, *Lysander*, 15.2.
11. Pausanias, *Description of Greece*, 3.8.6.
12. Goldsworthy, *The Punic Wars*, 156.
13. Hanson, *A War Like No Other*; Bagnall, *The Peloponnesian War*.
14. Kagan, *The Peloponnesian War*, 478–484.
15. Tritle, *A New History of the Peloponnesian War*, 217.
16. Pausanias, *Description of Greece*, 2.2.20.
17. Ibid., 3.8.6.
18. Plutarch, *Lysander*, 15.3.
19. Cartledge 1978 largely refutes the claim that Spartan *homoioi* were completely illiterate.
20. Polyaenus, *Stratagems*, 1.45.5.
21. Buck, *A History of Boeotia*, 145.
22. Xenophon, *Hellenica*, 2.2.20.
23. Ibid., 2.2.23.
24. Thuc. 1.1 (W).
25. Xenophon, *Hellenica*, 3.5.3.
26. Ibid., 7.5.26–27.
27. Homer, *Iliad*, 5.461.

CHAPTER 7

THUCYDIDES FOUND

"My work is not a piece of writing designed to meet the taste of an immediate public, but was done to last forever."[1]

—Thucydides

"Friend, if you are wise, take me in hand.
But if you are completely ignorant of the Muses,
throw away what you do not understand.
I am not accessible to everyone,
though a few have admired Thucydides,
the son of Olorus, a Kekropid by birth."[2]

—Byzantine inscription to Thucydides, c. 11th century.

To write about Thucydides is, in some ways, to sail for Syracuse. The task is vast—far greater than any author could anticipate—and the way strewn with obstacles. Upon reaching the subject, its size and scale are revealed to be intimidating, even to those thoroughly familiar with it. Engaging with Thucydides provides constant challenge and requires constant reappraisal. This is only appropriate. One of our core arguments throughout this book has been that Thucydides's *The History*, like any other work of seminal influence to scholarship, should be used as a beginning not as an end. We must embrace the complexity of Thucydides and admit that the lessons to be derived from studying his work should not be simplistic. They require additional attention if their most enduring character is to be apprehended. In some ways, it is ironic that a book so long admired for its complexity and near inscrutable sophistication should now be something of a poster child for the sound bite.[3]

As we described in the introduction, Thucydides is currently enjoying some of his widest acclaim yet. His work was the inspiration for a "case file" on great power wars at Harvard's Belfer Center. His ideas from *The History* are quoted in *The Atlantic*[4] and *The Wall Street Journal*.[5] He is the subject of scholarly books, journal articles, and editorials too numerous to list. He is on the floor of the US Capitol in the speeches of senators and congressmen.[6] He has found his way to the Oval Office, the boardroom, and the silver screen.[7] "Thucydides's Trap" was even used as the "Year in a word [sic]" by the *Financial Times* for 2018.[8]

While we confirmed the utility of some of the lessons often drawn from *The History*, we have also highlighted how selective quotations, distillations, and presentism can be serious obstacles. They not only inhibit our understanding of the subject but also derive flawed (and perhaps even dangerous) universal lessons. After more than two millennia, these shallow interpretations continue to tell us less about Thucydides's world or the common characteristics of international affairs and domestic politics and more about the biases and preoccupations of authors and readers.

Our argument here has been that his work is best approached as a tool for opening and sustaining debate rather than as an authoritative gospel to rigidly frame discussions in artificial straitjackets or to shut it down completely. By embracing complexity and context, it is easier to defy the tendency towards simplicity and to return deserved richness to Thucydides.

In this book, we have presented some of these artificial straitjackets and endeavored to untie them: the fallacies of bipolarity and hegemonic war, the insufficiency of systemic causes of war, the stylization of sea power versus land power, the motivation of undefined "fear," and the inadequacy of a "realism" where the strong do simply as they want and the weak must only suffer as a result. We have introduced alternative concepts which, although not sufficient in themselves, are more consonant with Thucydides's work as a whole and with his broader era. His work shows us the dynamics of multipolarity influenced by flexible alliances, foreign policy dictated, in part, by domestic politics, and domestic politics, in turn, governed by individual agency, choice, and the power of rhetoric. *The History* explores the fundamental complexity of measuring, comparing, or deploying power, the deeper and more particular meanings of fear, and the enduring considerations of balance in international politics.

We have derived seven lessons present throughout Thucydides's work and supported by the history that succeeded both his truncated book and the war he attempted to chronicle. We see that:

1) Power defies simple metrics and categorization. Those looking to measure it must consider its roots and its manifestations. They must test how those manifestations can influence events and particular circumstances. It is no simple thing for states to understand whether their tools are fit to purpose. Leaders must look for the true weaknesses within other states as they must acknowledge that often the roots of their own power carry within them weaknesses of their own.

2) Alliances are fluid and dynamic. Wise alliances can deter conflict, but provocative alignments can spark it. We also see that allies, even weaker allies, can pressure partners into conflict if the more powerful partner fears losing their ally more than entering a war.

3) The combination of fluid alliances and difficult-to-measure power means that structural explanations for state conflict are often unsatisfactory.

4) Fluidity in alliances endures before, during, and after particular conflict, meaning that diplomacy is a constant as states jockey for position. Fluid alliances often expand conflicts beyond their initial

scope. Realignments, in turn, can make it difficult to judge when one conflict ends and another begins.

5) Major power wars do not automatically result in more stable international systems. The war between Athens and Sparta did not leave a period of even greater stability in its wake. The winner is not necessarily better off than before the war began. This point should serve as a significant warning to any major power —revisionist challenger or established hegemon—who prepares to engage in a hegemonic war.

6) Structural theories, such as realism, have descriptive and explanatory value when reading Thucydides for useful, recurring variables in international relations. But realism, as a theory, is not a sufficient explanation for all outcomes. Choice matters; therefore decision-making—both content and process—matters. Political institutions matter. Norms and values matter. The crafting of and adherence to agreements matter. The interplay between domestic economy and foreign policy matters. Personalities, perceptions, and public opinion matter. To read Thucydides, or any other classic work, without using these many lenses is to miss essential richness in favor of false rigor.

7) A final lesson from reading *The History* is that one must be very careful drawing lessons from history. At various points during the war, events from the past (whether recent or distant) were used to give warning, to frame decisions, and to predict outcomes. In the same spirit, three assertions about the relevance of Thucydides's world occur again and again. First, that what happened in Thucydides's time recurred in the centuries since. Next, that what happened in Thucydides time is happening now. Third, that we can see the future unfolding in the same patterns that were evident during the Peloponnesian War. Such analogies are only useful insofar as they are accurate and not twisted to suit the present needs or biases of policymakers.

These lessons are hardly comprehensive. No single work can distill Thucydides, nor can any work engage with a substantive analysis of all the subjects he presents for consideration. It is also impossible to examine the entirety of the available secondary literature. Our work is hardly above reproach. No doubt, important sources have been dealt with insufficiently. We urge our readers to take up the tasks we have left undone and to start doing so by carefully reading—and rereading—Thucydides's original book.

Single theories derived from Thucydides can provide insights necessary for understanding and for action in international relations. However, no single lesson derived from that book or any other is, by itself, sufficient for policy making and theory building. Taken in isolation, individual theories cannot prescribe ways that allow us to eliminate or substantially reduce the risks inherent in devising strategies and making policy. But combined with other theories, applied as multiple lenses, drawing on the rich history of cases like those provided by Thucydides, they can provide us with richer and more illuminating insights.

Broader evidence and arguments derived from Thucydides, from writers who were his contemporaries, and from modern scholarship about the classical world can lead to new ideas and valuable debates that extend beyond the inadequate and dangerous limits of presentism. Episodes, and the debates that accompany them, may be easily distorted. They lose their value when treated in isolation. However, when viewed across time and enriched by context, valuable continuities—both in errors and in successes—prove to have greater utility. When read together, for example, the debate over Corcyra and the debate over Sicily provide a richer, more valuable picture of the challenges of decision making, the interplay between domestic and international politics, and the evolution—and, in some instances, the decline—of policy making, both in form and in content.[9]

In the past, those who read Thucydides were well aware of his complexity and warned readers about it. For five hundred years (ca. 800–1300 CE), Thucydides fell from favor among the Byzantine academics who had inherited the literary legacy of the ancient Greeks. Those with sufficiently arcane tastes still read him, of course. But they cautioned those who would follow in their footsteps, with a witty poem that soon became a commonplace inscription at the start of his work:

> *Friend, if you are wise, take me in hand*
>
> *But if you are completely ignorant of the Muses*
>
> *throw away what you do not understand*
>
> *I am not accessible to everyone.*[10]

Whether we hear the wry caution of the Byzantine scholars, or modern warnings to "stop reading Thucydides,"[11] to "handle him with care,"[12] or to avoid "abusing" him,[13] we must acknowledge Thucydides's enduring ability to both fascinate and frustrate.

Thucydides is just one in a long line of authors whose work has been misread, under-read, or unread. The words of contemporary scholars suffer the same fate. Their authors no doubt cringe when a talking head or a student misuses a well-worn phrase, like "where you stand depends on where you sit." Regardless of the author or their era, reshaping the past to legitimize the debates and opinions of the present weakens theory just as it poisons policy.

There are lessons that Thucydides can tell us if we embrace complexity. The greatest value is in reading this text richly with care taken and not with a narrow focus or through a distillation. At the same time, it is critical to guard against placing decisive weight on contemporary policy challenges in search of definitive analogies. Even the greatest works need cultural awareness, precise textual analysis, and context—broad historical context—both before and after the period they describe if we are to derive durable lessons.

The value of Thucydides endures. He presents us with a complex conception of power and challenges us to go beyond it, sidelining those who would engage in conflict based on a simple understanding of what makes states powerful. He offers us the frame of systemic explanations for behavior but exceeds this with powerful evidence about the importance of domestic actors, choice, human agency, and the power of leaders. He praises democratic reformers like Pericles while criticizing the tensions and troubles inherent in democracy and describing the virtues of oligarchy. He shows us humanity at its most vulnerable, most venal, and most cruel—humanity through a true mirror—yet so far from what we consider "human" virtue. He shows us humanity at its most ambitious, with the marvelous ambiguity the Greeks recognized in humanity and in human ambition. In Thucydides we see both the ambition for greatness, for beauty, and for achievement set out in the Funeral Oration of Pericles—the ambition for the excellence of the human spirit—but we also see the naked ambition for power and for control so evident in the grandiosity of Alcibiades and in the Athenian imperial project itself.

At the same time, Thucydides is not without his many, well-documented flaws. His own agendas are often detectable. His own context and experiences influenced his views on important subjects. Like all historians, he was a product of his environment and his education. At times, he was often forced to rely on second-hand records of events he could not witness and the actions of individuals he could not interrogate. We have no way of knowing how Thucydides would have concluded his history. With all his strength and all his weakness, Thucydides remains valuable to those willing to take the time to fully explore his writing. His original goal was to point future generations to reliable answers.

> It will be enough for me, however, if these words of mine are judged useful by those who want to understand clearly the events which happened in the past and which (human nature being what it is) will, at some time or other and in much the same ways, be repeated in the future.[14]

Ultimately, Thucydides is not a source of settled answers but of enduring questions. In his *Moralia*, Plutarch—the priest at Delphi whose writings are intellectual descendants of *The History*—contended that, "[t]he mind is not a vessel to be filled, but a fire to be kindled."[15] In that spirit, we should view Thucydides's writings as the beginning of debate, not its end.

Notes

1. Thuc. 1.22 (W).
2. Kennedy, "A Classic Dethroned," 633.
3. Part of this has to do with language. Thucydides's Greek is particularly complex (Warner 1954, 33). In previous generations, scholars had to navigate these treacherous waters for themselves. In our own time of abundant translations, such concerns are largely removed, and Thucydides is readily accessible in a host of languages. In whatever language, however, grappling with the myriad issues Thucydides presents remains a challenge for any reader.
4. Allison, "The Thucydides Trap" and Schake, "The Summer of Misreading Thucydides."
5. Epstein, "History Made by Men, Not Gods."
6. Sawyer, "Thucydides in Modern Political Rhetoric," in Lee and Morley Eds., *A Handbook to the Reception of Thucydides*.
7. Crowley, "Why the White House is Reading Greek History," Drezner, "The Good, the Bad and the Ugly Aspects of Thucydides in the Trump Administration," Vlahos, "Who did Thucydides Trap?"
8. Rachman, "Year in a Word," https://www.ft.com/content/0e4ddcf4-fc7 8-11e8-aebf-99e208d3e521.
9. Thuc. 1.88; 6.105.
10. Byzantine inscription to an edition of Thucydides, quoted in S. Kennedy, "A Classic Dethroned," 633.
11. Welch, "Why International Relations Theorists Should Stop Reading Thucydides."
12. Kirshner, "Handle Him with Care."
13. Bagby, "The Use and Abuse of Thucydides in International Relations," Kouskouvelis, *Thucydides on Choice and Decision Making*.
14. Thuc. 1.22.
15. Plutarch, *On Listening and Lectures*, 48c.

Bibliography

Ancient Texts

Aristophanes. *The Frogs and Other Plays.* Translated by David Barrett. New York: Penguin 2007.

Diodorus Siculus. *Library.* Translated by C.H. Oldfather. Cambridge: Harvard University Press, 1946.

Euripides. *The Plays.* Translated by Edward P. Coleridge. Chicago: William Benton, 1952.

Herodotus. *The Histories.* Translated by A.D. Godley. Cambridge: Cambridge University Press, 1920.

Pausanias. *Description of Greece,* Translated by W.H.S. Jones. Cambridge, MA: Harvard University Press, 1918.

Plato. *The Republic.* Translated by Desmond Lee. London: Penguin Books, 2003.

Plutarch. *The Rise and Fall of Athens: Nine Greek Lives.* Translated by Ian Scott-Kilvert. London: Penguin Books, 1960.

———. *Moralia.* Translated by Frank Babbitt. Cambridge: Harvard University Press, 1936.

Thucydides. *History of the Peloponnesian War* [1903]. Translated by Richard Crawley. Edited by R. Robert Conner. Rutland: Charles Tuttle, 1993. [Denoted "C" in notes and book.]

———. *The History,* Translated by Rex Warner. New York: Penguin Books, 1972. [Denoted "W" in notes and book.]

———. *The Peloponnesian War.* Translated by Martin Hammond. Oxford: Oxford University Press, 2009. [Denoted "H" in notes and book.]

———. *The War of the Peloponnesians and the Athenians.* Cambridge: Cambridge University Press, 2013.

Xenophon. *The Landmark Xenophon's Hellenika.* Translated by John Marincola. Edited by Robert B. Strassler, New York: Pantheon Books, 2009.

MODERN TEXTS

Allison, Graham. "The Thucydides Trap: Are the US and China Headed for Warj." *The Atlantic,* September 24, 2015.

———. *Destined for War: Can America and China Escape Thucydides's Trap.* New York: Houghton Mifflin Harcourt, 2017.

Aron, Raymond. *Peace and War: A Theory of International Relations.* New Brunswick, NJ: Transaction Publishers, 2009.

Art, Robert, and Robert Jervis. *International Politics: Enduring Concepts and Contemporary Issues,* 9th edition. New York: Pearson Longman, 2009.

Bagnall, Nigel. *The Peloponnesian War: Athens, Sparta, and the Struggle for Greece.* New York: Thomas Dunne Books, 2004.

Bedford, David, and Thom Workman. "The Tragic Reading of the Thucydides Tragedy." *Review of International Studies* 27, no. 1 (2001): 51–57.

Brands, Hall, and Jeremi Suri, eds. *The Power of the Past: History and Statecraft.* Washington, DC: Brookings Institution Press, 2015.

Buck, Robert J. *A History of Boeotia.* Edmonton: The University of Alberta Press, 1979.

Caldwell, Dan, and Robert E. Williams, Jr. *Seeking Security in an Insecure World.* Lanham: Rowman & Littlefield, 2006.

Cartledge, Paul, "Literacy in the Spartan Oligarchy." *The Journal of Hellenic Studies* 98 (1978): 25–37.

———. *Sparta and Lakonia: A Regional History 1300–362 BC.* Abingdon: Routledge, 2002.

———. *The Spartans: The World of the Warrior Heroes of Ancient Greece.* New York: Overlook Press, 2003.

Clinton, W. David, ed. *The Realist Tradition and Contemporary International Relations.* Louisiana: Louisiana State University Press, 2007.

Crowley, Michael. "Why the White House Is Reading Greek History." *Politico,* June 21, 2017, https://www.politico.com/magazine/story/2017/06/21/why-the-white-house-is-reading-greek-history-215287

Desmond, William. "Lessons of Fear: A Reading of Thucydides." *Classical Philology* 101 (2006): 359–79.

Dougherty, James E., and Robert L. Pfaltzgraff. *Contending Theories of International Relations: A Comprehensive Survey, 3rd Edition.* New York: Harper Collins, 1990.

Doyle, Michael. "Thucydidean Realism." *Review of International Studies* 16, no. 3 (1990): 223–237.

———. *Ways of War and Peace.* New York: W.W. Norton & Company, 1997.

Dunn, Tim, Milja Kurki, and Steve Smith. *International Relations Theories: Discipline and Diversity.* Oxford: Oxford University Press, 2007.

Drezner, Daniel. "The Good, the Bad and the Ugly Aspects of Thucydides in the Trump Administration." *The Washington Post,* June 22, 2017.

———. "Which Classic Work of International Relations Offers the Most Pertinent Description of Today?" *The Washington Post,* March 2, 2017.

Eckstein, Arthur M. *Mediterranean Anarchy, Interstate War, and the Rise of Rome.* Berkeley: University of California Press, 2006.

Fischer, David Hackett. *Historians' Fallacies: Toward a Logic of Historical Thought 1st Edition.* New York: Harper and Row, 1970.

Fleiss, Peter. *Thucydides and the Politics of Bipolarity.* Baton Rouge: Louisiana State University Press, 1966.

Forde, Steve. "Thucydides on Peace." In *The Realist Tradition and Contemporary International Relations,* edited by W. David Clinton. Baton Rouge: Louisiana State University Press, 2007.

Freedman, Lawrence. *Strategy.* Oxford: Oxford University Press, 2013.

Garst, Daniel. "Thucydides and Neorealism." *International Studies Quarterly* 33, no. 1 (1989): 3–27.

Goldsworthy, Adrian. *The Punic Wars.* London: Cassell, 2000.

Gilpin, Robert. *War and Change in World Politics.* Cambridge: Cambridge University Press, 1981.

———. "The Theory of Hegemonic War." *The Journal of Interdisciplinary History* 18, no. 4 (1988): 591–613.

———. "Peloponnesian and Cold War." In *Hegemonic Rivalry from Thucydides to the Nuclear Age,* edited by Richard Ned Lebow and Barry Strauss. Boulder: Westview Press, 1991.

Gustafson, Lowell, ed. *Thucydides' Theory of International Relations: A Lasting Possession.* Baton Rouge: Louisiana State University, 2000.

Handel, Michael I. *Masters of War: Classical Strategic Thought, 3ʳᵈ Edition.* London: Frank Cass, 2001.

Hanson, Victor Davis. *A War Like No Other.* New York: Random House, 2005.

Heathcote, Tony. *The British Admirals of the Fleet 1734–1995.* Barnsley: Leo Cooper, 2002.

Holsti, K. J. *The Dividing Discipline: Hegemony and Diversity in International Theory.* Winchester: Allen & Unwin, 1985.

Howard, Michael. *The Causes of Wars.* Cambridge: Harvard University Press, 1984.

Jaffe, S.N. *Thucydides on the Outbreak of War: Character and Contest.* Oxford: Oxford University Press, 2017.

Johnson-Bagby, Laurie M. "The Use and Abuse of Thucydides in International Relations." International Organization 48, no.1 (1994): 131–53.

Kagan, Donald. "Corinthian Diplomacy after the Peace of Nicias." *The American Journal of Philology* 81, no. 3 (1960): 291–310.

———. *The Fall of the Athenian Empire.* Ithaca: Cornell University Press, 1987.

———. *On the Origins of War and the Preservation of Peace.* New York: Anchor Books, 1995.

———. *The Peloponnesian War.* New York: Penguin, 2003.

———. *Thucydides: The Reinvention of History.* New York: Penguin, 2009.

Kaufman, Daniel, Jay M. Parker, and Kimberley Field. *Understanding International Relations: The Value of Alternative Lenses, 4th edition.* New York: McGraw-Hill, 1999.

Kauppi, Mark V. "Thucydides: Character and Capabilities." *Security Studies* 5, no. 2 (1995): 142–168.

Kennedy, Paul. *The Rise and Fall of the Great Powers.* New York: Random House, 1987.

Kennedy, Scott. "A Classic Dethroned: The Decline and Fall of Thucydides in Middle Byzantium." *Greek, Roman, and Byzantine Studies* 58 (2018): 607–635.

Khong, Yuen Foong. *Analogies at War: Korea, Munich, Dien Bien Phu, and the Vietnam Decisions of 1965.* Princeton: Princeton University Press, 1992.

Kirshner, Jonathan. "Handle Him with Care: The Importance of Getting Thucydides Right." *Security Studies* 28, no. 1 (2019).

Korab-Korpowicz, W. Julian. "How International Relations Theorists Can Benefit By Reading Thucydides." *The Monist* 89, no. 2 (2006): 231–244.

Kouskouvelis, Ilias. *Thucydides on Choice and Decision Making: Why War Is Not Inevitable.* Lanham: Lexington Books, 2019.

Lacey, James. *Great Strategic Rivalries: From the Classical World to the Cold War.* Oxford: Oxford University Press, 2016.

Lebow, Richard Ned, and Barry Strauss, eds. *Hegemonic Rivalry from Thucydides to the Nuclear Age.* Boulder: Westview Press, 1991.

Lebow, Richard Ned. *The Tragic Vision of Politics: Ethics, Interests and Orders.* Cambridge: Cambridge University Press, 2003.

———. "Thucydides and Deterrence." *Security Studies* 16, no. 2 (2007): 163–188.

———. "International Relations and Thucydides." In *Thucydides and the Modern World: Reception, Reinterpretation and Influence from the Re-*

naissance to the Present, edited by Neville Morley and Katherine Harloe, 197–211. Cambridge: Cambridge University Press, 2012.

Lee, Christine, and Neville Morley, eds. *A Handbook to the Reception of Thucydides*. New York: John Wiley and Sons, 2014.

Legon, Ronald P. "The Peace of Nicias." *Journal of Peace Research* 6, no. 4 (1969): 323–334.

Mackinder, Halford. "The Geographical Pivot of History (1904)." *The Geographical Journal* 23, no. 4 (2004): 298–321.

Mearsheimer, John. *The Tragedy of Great Power Politics*. New York: W.W. Norton, 2001.

Meier, Christian, and Robert Kimber. *Athens: A Portrait of a City in Its Golden Age*. London: John Murray, 1999.

Mendelsohn, Daniel. "Block That Metaphor! The Right Form." *The New Yorker*, July 27, 2015, 18–19.

Morley, Neville, and Katherine Harloe, eds. *Thucydides and the Modern World: Reception, Reinterpretation and Influence from the Renaissance to the Present*. Cambridge: Cambridge University Press, 2012.

Morley, Neville. "The Melian Dilemma: Remaking Thucydides." *Epoiesen: A Journal for Creative Engagement in History and Archaeology*, February 8, 2019, https://doi.org/10.22215/epoiesen/2019.2

Neustadt, Richard, and Ernest May. *Thinking in Time: The Uses of History for Decision-Makers 1st Edition*. New York: Free Press, 1988.

Nolan, Cathal J. *The Allure of Battle: A History of How Wars Have been Won and Lost*. New York: Oxford University Press, 2017.

Novo, Andrew R. "Where We Get Thucydides Wrong: The Fallacies of History's First 'Hegemonic' War." *Diplomacy & Statecraft* 27, no. 1 (2016): 1–21.

Nye, Joseph. *Soft Power: The Means to Success in World Politics*. New York: PublicAffairs, 2004.

———. *Understanding International Conflicts: An Introduction to Theory and History, 7th Edition*. New York: Pearson Longman, 2009.

Ober, Josiah. *Political Dissent in Democratic Athens: Intellectual Critics of Popular Rule*. Princeton: Princeton University Press, 1998.

Platias, Athanassios, and Constantinos Koliopoulos. "Grand Strategies Clashing: Athenian and Spartan Strategies in Thucydides' 'History of the Peloponnesian War.'" *Comparative Strategy* 21, 5 (2010): 377–399.

Rahe, Paul A. *The Spartan Regime: Its Character, Origins, and Grand Strategy*. New Haven: Yale University Press, 2016.

———. "The Primacy of Greece: Athens and Sparta." In *Great Strategic Rivalries: From the Classical World to the Cold War*, edited by James Lacey. Oxford: Oxford University Press, 2016.

Rawlings, Hunter R., Jacqueline de Romilly, Jeffrey S. Rusten, Elizabeth Rawlings, and Hunter R. Rawlings III. *The Mind of Thucydides*. Ithaca: Cornell University Press, 2017.

Rhodes, P.J. "Thucydides on the Causes of the Peloponnesian War." *Hermes* 115, no 2. (1987): 154–165.

Rochlin, James. "Critical Security in the 21st Century: The Resonating Voices of Thucydides." *Alternatives* 11, no. 1 (2012): 1–12.

Santoro, Carlo M. "Bipolarity and War." In *Hegemonic Rivalry from Thucydides to the Nuclear Age*, edited by Richard Ned Lebow and Barry Strauss. Boulder: Westview Press, 1991.

Schake, Kori. "The Summer of Misreading Thucydides." *The Atlantic*, July 18, 2017, https://www.theatlantic.com/international/archive/20 17/07/the-summer-of-misreading-thucydides/533859/

Schlosser, Joel Alden. "'Hope, Danger's Comforter': Thucydides, Hope, Politics." *The Journal of Politics* 75, no. 1 (2012): 169–182.

Schweller, Randall L., and William C. Wohlforth. "Power Test: Evaluation Realism in Response to the End of the Cold War." *Security Studies* 9, no. 3 (Spring 2000): 60–107.

Snyder, Glenn H. "The Security Dilemma in Alliance Politics." *World Politics* 36, no. 4, (1984): 461-495.

Sommerstein, Alan H., and Andrew Bayliss. *Oath and State in Ancient Greece*. Berlin: Walter de Gruyter, 2013.

Ste. Croix, G.E.M. de. "The Character of the Athenian Empire." *Histori: Zeitschrift Für Alte Geschichte* 3, no. 1 (1954): 1–41.

———. *The Origins of the Peloponnesian War.* Ithaca: Cornell University Press, 1972.

Thauer, Christian R., and Christian Wendt. *Thucydides and Political Order: Concepts of Order and the History of the Peloponnesian War.* New York: Palgrave Macmillan, 2016.

Tiezzi, Shannon. "US-China Relations: Thucydidean Trap or Prisoner's Dilemma?" *The Diplomat*, March 24, 2014, http://thediplomat.com/2014/03

Tsakiris, Theodore George. "Thucydides and Strategy: Formations of Grand Strategy in the History of the Second Peloponnesian War (431–404 B.C.)." *Comparative Strategy* 25, no. 3 (2006): 173–208.

Tritle, Lawrence A. *A New History of the Peloponnesian War.* Oxford: Wiley & Blackwell, 2010.

Turner, Stansfield. "Address to Chicago Council Navy League of the United States Lake Shore Club." March 9, 1973, https://www.cia.gov/library/readingroom/docs/CIA-RDP80B01554R003500280001-7.pdf

Twain, Mark, and Charles Dudley Warner. *The Gilded Age: A Tale of Today.* Mineola, New York: Dover Publications, Inc., 2020.

Viotti, Paul R., and Mark V. Kauppi. *International Relations Theory: Realism, Pluralism, Globalism, and Beyond.* Boston: Allyn and Bacon 1999.

Vlahos, Michael. "Who did Thucydides Trap?" *The American Conservative*, July 5, 2017.

Waltz, Kenneth N. *Man, the State, and War: A Theoretical Analysis.* New York: Columbia University Press, 1954.

———. "The Stability of a Bipolar World." *Daedalus* 93, no. 3, 1964.

———. *Theory of International Politics.* Reading: Addison-Wesley Press, 1979.

Wasserman, Felix Martin. "The Melian Dialogue." *Transactions and Proceedings of the American Philological Association* 78 (1947): 18–36.

Welch, David A. "Why International Relations Theorists Should Stop Reading Thucydides." *Review of International Studies* 29, no. 3 (2003): 301–319.

Wohlforth, William. "The Stability of a Unipolar World." *International Security* 24, no. 1 (1999): 5–41.

Zagorin, Perez. *Thucydides: An Introduction For the Common Reader.* Princeton: Princeton University Press, 2005.

Zongyou, Wei. "China-US Relations: The Myth of the Thucydides Trap." *The Diplomat*, March 30, 2014, http://thediplomat.com/2014/03

INDEX

About the Authors

Andrew R. Novo is an associate professor of strategic studies at the National Defense University in Washington, DC. He holds a D.Phil and M.Phil from the University of Oxford and an AB from Princeton University. Dr. Novo's previous publications include *When Small Countries Crash* and *Queen of Cities*. He has published in several journals such as *Diplomacy & Statecraft* and *The Journal of Modern Greek Studies* as well as in the *Harvard International Review* and the *New Atlanticist*. Dr. Novo delivered the inaugural "Thucydides Lecture" at the University of Macedonia (Thessaloniki, Greece) in January 2019 and has also presented at the Brookings Institution and the Atlantic Council.

Jay M. Parker is Distinguished Professor and Major General Fox Conner Chair of International Security Studies at the College of International Security Affairs, National Defense University in Washington, D.C. His previous academic experience includes service as Professor and Director of International Relations and National Security Studies at the United States Military Academy (West Point). Dr. Parker also taught at Georgetown University, George Washington University, and Columbia University, and he was a visiting research fellow at Princeton University and at Japan's National Institute for Defense Studies. He has published and presented on East Asian security, U.S. foreign policy, presidential decision making, and mass media. A graduate of the University of Arizona, he earned master's degrees from Arizona State University, University of Southern California, and U.S. Naval War College, and a PhD in political science from Columbia University.

CAMBRIA RAPID COMMUNICATIONS IN CONFLICT AND SECURITY (RCCS) SERIES

General Editor: Geoffrey R. H. Burn

The aim of the RCCS series is to provide policy makers, practitioners, analysts, and academics with in-depth analysis of fast-moving topics that require urgent yet informed debate. Since its launch in October 2015, the RCCS series has the following book publications:

- *A New Strategy for Complex Warfare: Combined Effects in East Asia* by Thomas A. Drohan
- *US National Security: New Threats, Old Realities* by Paul R. Viotti
- *Security Forces in African States: Cases and Assessment* edited by Paul Shemella and Nicholas Tomb
- *Trust and Distrust in Sino-American Relations: Challenge and Opportunity* by Steve Chan
- *The Gathering Pacific Storm: Emerging US-China Strategic Competition in Defense Technological and Industrial Development* edited by Tai Ming Cheung and Thomas G. Mahnken
- *Military Strategy for the 21st Century: People, Connectivity, and Competition* by Charles Cleveland, Benjamin Jensen, Susan Bryant, and Arnel David
- *Ensuring National Government Stability After US Counterinsurgency Operations: The Critical Measure of Success* by Dallas E. Shaw Jr.
- *Reassessing U.S. Nuclear Strategy* by David W. Kearn, Jr.
- *Deglobalization and International Security* by T. X. Hammes
- *American Foreign Policy and National Security* by Paul R. Viotti

- *Make America First Again: Grand Strategy Analysis and the Trump Administration* by Jacob Shively

- *Learning from Russia's Recent Wars: Why, Where, and When Russia Might Strike Next* by Neal G. Jesse

- *Restoring Thucydides: Testing Familiar Lessons and Deriving New Ones* by Andrew R. Novo and Jay M. Parker

- *Net Assessment and Military Strategy: Retrospective and Prospective Essays* edited by Thomas G. Mahnken, with an introduction by Andrew W. Marshall

For more information, visit www.cambriapress.com.